Writing Program Administration

Journal of the
Council of Writing Program Administrators

Editors
Barbara L'Eplattenier .... University of Arkansas at Little Rock
Sherry Rankins-Robertson .... University of Arkansas at Little Rock
Lisa Mastrangelo .... Centenary College of New Jersey

Assistant Editors
Sarah Ricard .... University of Arkansas at Little Rock
Catherine Godlewsky .... Centenary College of New Jersey
Jonathen Munoz .... Centenary College of New Jersey

Book Review Editor
Norbert Elliot .... New Jersey Institute of Technology

Associate Book Review Editor
Jacob Babb .... Indiana University Southeast

Ads Manager
Kelsie Walker .... Ball State University

Editorial Board
Bradley Bleck .... Spokane Falls Community College
Micheal Callaway .... Mesa Community College
Norbert Elliot .... New Jersey Institute of Technology
Casie Fedukovich .... North Carolina State University
Tarez Samra Graban .... Florida State University
Kristine Hansen .... Brigham Young University
Al Harahap .... University of Arizona, WPA-GO Representative
Asao B. Inoue .... University of Washington, Tacoma
Seth Kahn .... West Chester University
Carrie Leverenz .... Texas Christian University
Paul Kei Matsuda .... Arizona State University
Mark McBeth .... John Jay College of Criminal Justice/CUNY
Laura Micciche .... University of Cincinnati
Charles Paine .... University of New Mexico
E. Shelley Reid .... George Mason University
Rochelle (Shelley) Rodrigo .... Old Dominion University
Ellen Schendel .... Grand Valley State University
Wendy Sharer .... East Carolina University
Amy Ferdinandt Stolley .... Saint Xavier University
Martha A. Townsend .... University of Missouri
Elizabeth Vander Lei .... Calvin College
Scott Warnock .... Drexel University

WPA: Writing Program Administration is published twice per year—fall and spring—by the Council of Writing Program Administrators. Production and printing of *WPA: Writing Program Administration* is managed by Parlor Press.

Council of Writing Program Administrators

Executive Board

The Council of Writing Program Administrators is a national association of college and university faculty who serve or have served as directors of first-year composition or writing programs, coordinators of writing centers and writing workshops, chairpersons and members of writing-program-related committees, or in similar administrative capacities. The Council of Writing Program Administrators is an affiliate of the Association of American Colleges and the Modern Language Association.

Susan Miller-Cochran, President .... University of Arizona
Dominic DelliCarpini, Vice President .... York College of Pennsylvania
Rita Malenczyk, Past President .... Eastern Connecticut State University
Nicholas Behm .... Elmhurst College
Peter Gray .... Queensborough Community College/CUNY
Amy Kimme Hea .... University of Arizona
Mark Blaauw-Hara .... North Central Michigan College
Heidi Estrem .... Boise State University
Tracy Morse .... East Carolina University
Asao Inoue .... University of Washington-Tacoma
Karen Keaton Jackson .... North Carolina Central University
Cheri Lemieux-Spiegel .... Northern Virginia Community College

Ex-Officio

Christine Cucciarre, Treasurer .... University of Delaware
Michael McCamley, Secretary .... University of Delaware
Shirley K Rose, Director, Consultant Evaluator Service ... Arizona State University
Michael Pemberton .... Georgia Southern University
    Associate Director, Consultant Evaluator Service
Barbara L'Eplattenier, Journal Editor .... University of Arkansas at Little Rock
Lisa Mastrangelo, Journal Editor .... Centenary College of New Jersey
Sherry Rankins-Robertson, Journal Editor ... University of Arkansas at Little Rock
Kat Daily O'Meara, WPA-GO .... Arizona State University
Virginia Schwarz, Vice Chair, WPA-GO .... University of Wisconsin-Madison

Authors' Guide

WPA: Writing Program Administration publishes empirical and theoretical research on issues in writing program administration. We publish a wide range of research in various formats, research that not only helps both titled and untitled administrators of writing programs do their jobs, but also helps our discipline advance academically, institutionally, and nationally. *WPA: Writing Program Administration* is published twice per year: fall and spring. Possible topics of interest include:

- writing faculty professional development
- writing program creation and design
- critical analysis and applications of discipline or national policies and statements that impact writing programs
- labor conditions: material, practical, fiscal
- WAC/WID/WC/CAC (or other sites of communication/writing in academic settings)
- teaching multimodal writing
- teaching in digital spaces
- theory, practice, and philosophy of writing program administration
- outreach and advocacy
- writing program assessment
- WPA history and historical work
- national and regional trends in education and their impact on WPA work
- issues of professional advancement and writing program administration
- diversity and WPA work
- writing programs in a variety of educational locations (SLAC, HBCU, two-year colleges, Hispanic schools, non-traditional schools, concurrent work)
- interdisciplinary work that informs WPA practices

This list is not comprehensive. If you have questions about potential work for *WPA: Writing Program Administration*, please query the editors. We are particularly interested in publishing new voices and new topics.

Submission Guidelines

Check the website for complete submissions guidelines. Please include the cover sheet available at http://wpacouncil.org/info-for-authors. In general submissions should:

- be between 3,000–7,000 words; longer and shorter pieces will rarely be considered
- follow *MLA Style Manual and Guide to Scholarly Publishing* (most current edition)

- have identifying information removed for peer review: author name(s), track changes, comments, and properties cleared throughout
- include a short running head with page numbers
- include an abstract (200 words max) as part of the manuscript, following the title and preceding the body of the text
- have an accurate and correctly formatted works cited page
- include the cover sheet
- be saved as a .doc, .docx, or .rtf file. Do not send .pdf files. If you have special formatting needs, contact the editors.

More information regarding the formatting of the manuscript (specifically endnotes, tables, and pictures) is available at http://wpacouncil.org/node/1812. Manuscripts that don't conform to the requirements will be returned to the author with a request to reformat.

Reviews

WPA: Writing Program Administration publishes review essays of books related to writing programs and their administration. Publishers are invited to recommend appropriate books to bookreviews@wpacouncil.org. If you are interested in reviewing texts, please contact the book review editor at bookreviews@wpacouncil.org

Announcements and Calls

Relevant announcements and calls for papers and/or conference participation will be published as space permits. Announcements should not exceed 500 words, and calls for proposals/participation should not exceed 1,000 words. Please include contact information and links for further information. Submission deadlines in calls should be no earlier than January 1 for the fall/winter issue and June 1 for the spring issue. Please email your calls and announcements to journal@wpacouncil.org and include the text both in the body of the message and as an MS Word or RTF attachment.

Correspondence

Correspondence relating to the journal, submissions, or editorial issues should be sent to journal@wpacouncil.org

Subscriptions

WPA: Writing Program Administration is published twice per year—fall and spring by the Council of Writing Program Administrators. Members of the Council of Writing Program Administrators receive a subscription to the journal as part of their membership. Join at http://wpacouncil.org/join-renew. Active members have access to online versions of current and past issues through the WPA website http:wpacouncil.org/journalarchives. Library subscription information is available at http://wpacouncil.org/library-memberships.

Writing Program Administration

Journal of the
Council of Writing Program Administrators
Volume 39.2 (Spring 2016)

Contents

Letter from the Editors 7

Symposium: Challenging Whiteness and/in Writing Program Administration and Writing Programs 9

"Rhonda Left Early to Go to Black Lives Matter": Programmatic Support for Graduate Writers of Color 10
   Jasmine Kar Tang and Noro Andriamanalina

A Story-less Generation: Emergent WPAs of Color and the Loss of Identity through Absent Narratives 16
   Sherri Craig

Troubling the Boundaries Revisited: Moving Towards Change as Things Stay the Same 20
   Collin Lamont Craig and Staci M. Perryman-Clark

Notes on Race in Transnational Writing Program Administration .. 26
   Amy A. Zenger

Sustaining Balance: Writing Program Administration and the Mentorship of Minority College Students 31
   Regina McManigell Grijalva

WPA and the New Civil Rights Movement 36
   Genevieve García de Müeller

The Yardstick of Whiteness in Composition Textbooks 42
   Cedric D. Burrows

The Role of Composition Programs in De-Normalizing Whiteness in the University: Programmatic Approaches to Anti-Racist Pedagogies 47
   James Chase Sanchez and Tyler S. Branson

On Keeping Score: Instructors' vs. Students'
Rubric Ratings of 46,689 Essays 53
    Joseph M. Moxley and David Eubanks

Taming Big Data through Agile Approaches to Instructor Training
and Assessment: Managing Ongoing Professional Development in
Large First-Year Writing Programs 81
    Susan M. Lang

An Institutional Ethnography of Information Literacy Instruction:
Key Terms, Local/Material Contexts, and Instructional Practice.......105
    Michelle LaFrance

Travelogue

Aspen and Honeysuckle: How Faculty Development for Teaching
Writing Grows (Interview with Jessie Moore and Chris Anson) 124
    Shirley K Rose

Reviews

A New Perspective on Language-Level Writing Instruction 140
    Anne Ruggles Gere

Writing Majors: Signs of Things to Come.. 146
    T J Geiger II

Online Writing Instruction Principles and Practices:
Now Is the Future..152
    Elizabeth A. Monske

A Bird's Eye View of WAC in Practice: WAC Writing Assignments
at 100 Colleges and Universities 160
    Emily Isaacs

Letter from the Editors

Dear Readers,

We welcome you to the journal's Spring 2016 issue. Once again, we are pleased to bring you an issue filled with a variety of materials: articles, a symposium, our annual Travelogue, and book reviews.

We open the issue with a Symposium on Challenging Whiteness and/in Writing Program Administration and Writing Programs. From the rich submissions we received, we selected seven to be published. These submissions cover a variety of topics, addressing race-based issues pertaining to WPA work such as supporting faculty and graduate students in writing studies, choosing textbooks, de-normalizing whiteness, and in general, becoming more thoughtful and attentive to issues of race as administrators. Although some of the authors have published in these pages before, most are new to these pages, and we look forward to their continued contributions to the field of Writing Studies and writing program administration.

In a happy coincidence, two of our articles explore how big data can help us become better teachers and administrators. Joe Moxley and Dave Eubanks' "On Keeping Score: Instructors' vs. Students' Rubric Ratings of 46,689 Essays" investigates the effectiveness of having students score one another's intermediate essay drafts and explores the correlation between student ratings and instructor ratings; as the title states, the study draws its conclusion from 46,689 reviews of student papers from 482 sections of composition.

Similarly, Susan Lang's "Taming Big Data through Agile Approaches to Instructor Training and Assessment: Managing Ongoing Professional Development in Large First-Year Writing Programs" shows us how big data can help us provide better support and professional training to our teachers. Using concepts such as big data and agile taken from information technology, Lang explores ways that WPAs make our own work more productive, responsive, and fulfilling for teachers.

Finally, Michelle LaFrance's "An Institutional Ethnography of Information Literacy Instruction: Key Terms, Local/Material Contexts, and

Instructional Practice" moves us in a different direction as she explores the use of the term *information literacy* on campuses. LaFrance's work finds that most WPAs and instructors define the term on a highly individualized—and often radically different—basis. This creates tension in the way that assignments and methods of research are conceptualized and taught.

As has been the tradition for the past few years, Shirley K Rose interviewed Chris Anson and Jessie Moore, two of the local hosts for the upcoming WPA conference in Raleigh, North Carolina, for the Travelogue. The 2016 conference will be a joint hosting effort between two institutions and the regional Carolinas WPA affiliate, reflected in the conference's theme of "Engaging Multiple Perspectives in and about Writing Program Administration." We hope you enjoy the Travelogue as a preview to the conference.

The book review section closes the journal. Once again, Norbert Elliott and Jacob Babb have selected books for review that will inform and enhance the work of WPAs. We hope you enjoy them. At any time, feel free to contact Norbert and Jacob at bookreviews@wpacouncil.org.

Much unseen labor goes into the production of the journal, and copyediting is perhaps one of the most important but least recognized. Joel Wingard has consistently been kind enough to provide volunteer copyediting at the proof stage, and we remain immensely grateful to him. Alora D. Crooms provided fresh eyes at the final stages, and Sarah Ricard continues to assist us at every stage of production, tracking down questions on obscure style and copyediting-related topics. Lastly, student interns Catherine Godlewsky and Jonathen Munoz helped with odd tasks and formatting issues, for which we offer them our thanks. We also extend our gratitude to our ads manager, Kelsie Walker.

We hope to see you at the CWPA conference, and we'd love to talk with you. As always, please don't hesitate to contact us with ideas or concerns. Our email is journal@wpacouncil.org.

—Barb, Lisa, and Sherry

Symposium: Challenging Whiteness and/in Writing Program Administration and Writing Programs

In the Fall of 2015, in tandem with the CWPA Executive Board's call for an increased commitment to diversity, we issued a CFP for a Symposium on Challenging Whiteness and/in Writing Program Administration and Writing Programs.

The violence in Ferguson and DC; the creation of #blacklivesmatter; the killings of Trayvon Martin, Tamir Rice, Ramarley Graham, Freddie Gray, Sean Bell, Jonathan Ferrell, Darius Simmons, Ernest Hoskins and Oscar Grant; the deaths of Sandra Bland, Kindra Chapman, Joyce Curnell, Ralkina Jones and Raynette Turner while in police custody brought national attention to the realities of majority minority citizens in this country. We call out these names to remind us that many of us are able to turn our heads and close the doors, as our privilege allows, to these injustices. All too often we forget the names of these individuals because our communities, our cultures, our families, and our homes are not subject to the violence of racial intolerance.

This symposium is one attempt to provide a place—both physical and intellectual—to keep looking, to keep the door open, to keep the conversation going and to keep learning.

We spent a fair amount of time deliberating with our Editorial Board about the merits and disadvantages of a special issue versus a symposium, despite our first instinct to do a special issue. A special issue, to be sure, marks the topic in ways that a symposium can't—a full issue dedicated to a single topic draws attention in a way that is difficult to do otherwise. For us, however, the significant disadvantage to a special issue was the time it would take to put together a special issue: a minimum of one and a half to two years. Steps such as issuing a call for proposals, getting manuscripts, editing and revising manuscripts, and copyediting do not happen quickly. A symposium, on the other hand, could move more swiftly (well, as swiftly as the academic publishing cycle can move); we issued the call for proposals for the Symposium in September of 2015 and are publishing the responses less than a year later.

We chose seven pieces to be published from the submissions, all of which drove home to us the diversity of our discipline, the many ways it is possible (and needed) to challenge whiteness, and the multiple ways it is possible to work towards social justice. We are grateful to the authors for expressing their perspectives and sharing critical scholarship relevant to the work of WPAs. We have enjoyed working with the authors on their pieces, and we look forward continuing to hearing their voices in our disciplinary conversations.

We hope you find the conversations here thought-provoking and practical, theoretical and useful, and a call to action in the same way we did.

"Rhonda Left Early to Go to Black Lives Matter": Programmatic Support for Graduate Writers of Color

Jasmine Kar Tang and Noro Andriamanalina

Benignly, it seems, this handwritten sentence exists on our Shut Up and Write retreat's Wall of Accomplishments, nestled amidst other statements (e.g., "90% done with diss proposal!", "finished coding two interviews").[1] The sentence stands out to us, and, as administrators/researchers, we are intrigued by a few things: that a student found value in documenting Rhonda's decision to end her retreat early; that on first thought, the statement has nothing to do with a so-called writing accomplishment; and that this statement reflects the work of our relatively new Writing Initiative housed in the graduate diversity office on our campus.

Our writing program—and this article—acknowledge that race and writing are inextricable: Racial formation cannot be removed from writing program administration in the US nation-state.[2] We need a hard look at what it would mean to support graduate writers of color at the programmatic level.[3] Pointedly, this isn't about promoting what Chandra Mohanty calls the "Race Industry" in which racial difference becomes managed and subsumed by the institution (196). We argue for a comprehensive writing program for graduate students of color that is defined by the following: 1) equal emphasis on research and practice on the part of the WPA, especially with respect to local contexts and histories of communities of color;[4] 2) acknowledgement of how non-mainstream epistemologies connect to writing practice; 3) relatedly, recognition that for many students of color, connection to community is inseparable from one's academic identity;[5] and 4) the integration of writing support in a robust, institutional effort that focuses on the academic and personal well-being of graduate students of color.

THEY MUST HAVE A LOT OF LANGUAGE ISSUES

At a Research 1 institution like the University of Minnesota, the student community is as heterogeneous as it is disparate. With a campus of nearly 50,000 students, it is easy (and perhaps likely) for members of the university community to feel like a number, to be lost in the red tape of a campus large enough that you might need to walk across the Mississippi River to get to your next class. If you are a person of color at this historically white institution (82% white), your numeric minority status can add another layer to the impersonal nature of the place. Further, if you are a person of color in a graduate program, the percentage declines from 18% to 3.5% of the total student body.

"I work with a writing program in the Office for Diversity in Graduate Education," one of us recently told a white female colleague. "Oh, that's important. The students must have a lot of language issues." As the exchange progressed, it was revealed that by language issues, our colleague wasn't referring to the challenge that graduate students have with navigating disciplinary writing expectations.[6] She was assuming that the students with whom we work are not US born, and—to use the outdated moniker—ESL. This exchange is emblematic of the circumstances and ideologies that concern and surround many people of color, regardless of citizenship or language status.

Studies of graduate students of color paint a bleak picture, citing racial isolation and racial microaggressions as part of the everyday experiences of this student community.[7] Gildersleeve, Croom, and Vasquez also identify what they call the "Am I going crazy?!" narrative, "a racialized social narrative . . . that reveals the harmful institutional and systemic factors contributing to the possible derailment of Latina/o and Black doctoral students" (94). In addition, too often at large universities where graduate student resources are decentralized, student success relies on individual connections and relationships. To reduce the sense of racial isolation and to address the fact that support should not rely on such individual networks, our university established a central unit called the Community of Scholars Program (COSP) in 1998, providing academic and professional development support across academic disciplines for graduate students of color who are US citizens and permanent residents. Since its inception, COSP has expanded to involve numerous workshops, fellowships, mentoring and research opportunities, and, within the past two years, a Writing Initiative to provide resources to aid in degree completion and to build community among those in the writing stages of the thesis/dissertation. The Initiative involves writing workshops, individual consultations, writing groups, retreats, and a research project that features focus groups and interviews in which doctoral writers of color reveal to us their experiences navigating academic spaces and writing conventions. To use the language of the *WPA: Writing Program Administration* symposium call for proposals, the Writing Initiative challenges whiteness head on: We are guided by the philosophy that writing is an embodied practice in which personal experiences and background inform one's approach to researching and writing in the academy. Resources and programming are only available to graduate students of color, facilitating the possibility of (what students report as) writing and thinking in spaces where being a person of color is the norm. We lead a program that responds to the need to carve out, as one student puts it, an "ideological and physical space" for graduate writers of color.

I Don't Trust the Space

This sentence from a focus group transcript gets louder and louder the more we hear from student research subjects. The speaker here refers to the physical site of the graduate seminar classroom and the ideological site of academia at the doctoral level. She continues, "I don't trust the space to give it my genuine voice. . . . It is a little bit about, in my case, policing my own voice and then being careful about what I put out there." We wonder: What is the cost of leaving your voice and parts of your identity at the door? What does this mean for one's writing? How do we as writing program administrators mount an institutional "critique for" bringing one's whole, embodied self to the writing (Diab, Ferrel, Godbee, and Simpkins)?

We like to think that beginning a writing program in the atypical location of a diversity office is one approach. Our unit began by doing what many offices and departments on a college campus do: We outsourced our writing needs by asking for assistance from the writing center. We trust our readers to be familiar with this framework of "leaving the teaching of writing to the writing experts." Perhaps analogously, addressing diversity gets outsourced, too, when a unit on campus participates in a one-time workshop on race, facilitated by diversity office staff, therefore "leaving the teaching of race to the race experts." Doing so trivializes racial difference and does not get at institutional change, for the work of writing and the work of race should be a sustained effort undertaken in collaboration across campus units, disciplines, and communities. We want to trouble these parallel phenomena of outsourcing and bring them in conversation with one another—to have a program that not only recognizes the relationship between race and writing but also recognizes the great potential and the synergy produced when placing race and writing side-by-side on a programmatic level.

The result would be a writing program that takes up writing as an embodied act and that recognizes a multiplicity of personal and community histories and epistemologies and how they are tied up in racial formation. For example, we are continuously surprised by student evaluations of our monthly Shut Up and Write retreats. Limited to 15 participants, it is one of our most well-attended events, for in a predominantly white university that's the size of a small town, we can offer an intimate writing space. A participant reflects:

> To me, my own identity is really complicated and really personal. And I don't feel comfortable sharing it in this space. Well, *this* space is great, but I mean, like, in the university space, right? And actually that's why I really appreciate the Community of Scholars Program. It's great to be able to sit and write with others. I don't know them personally, maybe, but I know, I can sense some sort of shared understanding, right, that doesn't necessarily have to be verbal. But the fact that we can sit together and write, have it be a work space and support each other in producing our work and writing—that's really valuable.

Here the student names an intangible "shared understanding" that comes out of having a physical writing space for graduate students of color. Our program's individual writing consultations may be an alternative or supplement to what a research subject described as a "deracinated" writing center that exists "in a vacuum": The writing center "doesn't talk about language . . . It's just like this place, this block that writing happens, and you get help. *You* get help. *You*, this unmarked body." Our intervention is to have a writing program that centers equity and embodiment, with a focus on racialized communities and the histories and experiences that inform their/our work.

Justice for Jamar

This past winter, a protest called 4th Precinct ShutDown developed a few miles northeast of our campus. Community members, including Black Lives Matter organizers, camped out at a police station in protest of the circumstances surrounding the death of Jamar Clark, a 24-year-old African American man shot in the head by a police officer in November 2015 ("What We Know"). 4th Precinct ShutDown was eventually forcibly shut down itself, with law enforcement and city officials evicting protesters and tearing down the site after 18 days of peaceful occupation (the exception being the shooting of five protesters by masked civilians) (Golden; Williams). Justice for Jamar was the leading story on the local news for weeks, and Black Lives Matter continues to make headlines in the Twin Cities in a number of ways, including highly visible events at the Mall of America and the Minneapolis-St. Paul International Airport. The circumstances of Clark's death continue to be in dispute.

"Minneapolis and Ferguson are more similar than you think," *The Washington Post* reports, with a racial climate disguised by the calm surface of white liberalism (Guo). When we picture our college campus, the Justice for Jamar protest signs and banners seem distant. The university—pristine, untouchable, reflecting a whiteness in numbers, despite the diverse racial make-up of our city—seems disconnected from something like ShutDown or a protest at the largest mall in the country. Within the university, in the daily goings-on of, say, a writing program, Justice for Jamar may appear incongruent, unbelonging. WPAs may ask, "What does Black Lives Matter have to do with our work?" To say that racial justice is peripheral to WPA work would ignore the realities faced by student writers. We need to listen and learn from—and with—the voices and epistemologies of historically underrepresented communities. Our research among graduate writers of color reveals that what happens nationally, let alone what takes place locally in their own backyard, can directly affect them—and often cannot be separated from their writing as they progress through a graduate program. For many, their ties to community are intimately connected to academic life. We need to talk to graduate writers of color and understand the dynamics that are particular to our local contexts. We need to get a pulse on the racial climate of a place, for interrogating race and writing/WPA does not involve a one-size-fits-all model. A comprehensive model of support must involve equal attention to theory and practice. We call for WPAs to employ research and practice that unapologetically center race and writing.

Notes

1. Name has been changed. The IRB number is 1410E54662.

2. Racial formation is "the sociohistorical process by which racial categories are created, inhabited, transformed, and destroyed" (Omi and Winant 55).

3. When we refer to people of color, we include African American, American Indian, Asian American, and Latina/o communities.

4. See Poe's discussion of race and writing across the curriculum in which she makes the case for "situating race locally" (5).

5. Delgado Bernal challenges readers to consider the "critical raced-gendered epistemologies" that students of color bring to higher education (105).

6. See Brooks-Gillies, Garcia, Kim, Manthey, and Smith for a discussion of the contexts and needs of graduate writers.

7. See, for example, Gay; Lewis, Ginsberg, Davies, and Smith; and Solórzano.

Works Cited

Brooks-Gillies, Marilee, Elena G. Garcia, Soo Hyon Kim, Katie Manthey, and Trixie Smith. "Graduate Writing Across the Disciplines, Introduction." Spec. issue of *Across the Disciplines* 12.3 (2015). Web. 29 Nov. 2015.

Delgado Bernal, Dolores. "Critical Race Theory, Latino Critical Theory, and Critical Raced-gendered Epistemologies: Recognizing Students of Color as Holders and Creators of Knowledge." *Qualitative Inquiry* 8.1 (2002): 105–26. Print.

Diab, Rasha, Thomas Ferrel, Beth Godbee, and Neil Simpkins. "Making Commitments to Racial Justice Actionable." *Across the Disciplines* 10.3 (2013). Web. 16 April 2016.

Gay, Geneva. "Navigating Marginality en Route to the Professoriate: Graduate Students of Color Learning and Living in Academia." *International Journal of Qualitative Studies in Education* 17.2 (2004): 265–88. Print.

Gildersleeve, Ryan Evely, Natasha N. Croom, and Philip L. Vasquez. "'Am I Going Crazy?!': A Critical Race Analysis of Doctoral Education." *Equity and Excellence in Education* 44.1 (2011): 93–114. Print.

Golden, Erin. "Protesters Rally at City Hall after Minneapolis Police Clear Fourth Precinct Encampment." *Minneapolis Star Tribune* 4 Dec. 2015. Web. 12 Feb. 2016.

Guo, Jeff. "Why Minneapolis and Ferguson Are More Similar than You Think." *Washington Post* 24 Nov. 2015. Web. 30 Nov. 2015.

Lewis, Chance W., Rick Ginsberg, Tim Davies, and Kent Smith. "The Experiences of African American PhD Students at a Predominately White Carnegie I Research Institution." *College Student Journal* 38.2 (2004): 231–45. Print.

Mohanty, Chandra Talpade. *Feminism without Borders: Decolonizing Theory, Practicing Solidarity.* Durham: Duke UP, 2003. Print.

Omi, Michael, and Howard Winant. *Racial Formation in the United States: From the 1960s to the 1990s.* 2nd ed. New York: Routledge, 1994. Print.

Poe, Mya. "Re-framing Race in Teaching Writing across the Curriculum." *Across the Disciplines* 10.3 (2013): n. pag. Web. 30 Nov. 2015.

Solórzano, Daniel G. "Critical Race Theory, Race and Gender Microaggressions, and the Experience of Chicana and Chicano Scholars." *International Journal of Qualitative Studies in Education* 11.1 (1998): 121–36. Web. 29 March 2016.

"What We Know about the Death of Jamar Clark." *Minneapolis Star Tribune* 25 Nov. 2015. Web. 30 Nov. 2015.

Williams, Brandt. "5 People Shot at Black Lives Matter Protest in Minneapolis." National Public Radio. 24 Nov. 2015. Web. 14 Feb. 2016.

Jasmine Kar Tang is Postdoctoral Associate and Writing Initiative Coordinator with the Office for Diversity in Graduate Education at the University of Minnesota, a Research 1 institution. Her research interests include writing studies and critical race and ethnic studies. She is committed to enacting equitable and accessible administrative and pedagogical practices especially with respect to communities of color and multilingual communities. Jasmine is also co-principal investigator with Noro Andriamanalina on a study examining the strengths and challenges of doctoral writers of color.

Noro Andriamanalina earned her doctoral degree in educational policy and administration from the University of Minnesota, a Research 1 institution, where she is also Director of Academic and Professional Development for the Office for Diversity in Graduate Education. She is responsible for developing and evaluating programs to assist graduate students through the thesis/dissertation writing process while connecting them to research, teaching, and community engagement opportunities.

A Story-less Generation: Emergent WPAs of Color and the Loss of Identity through Absent Narratives

Sherri Craig

Storytelling, an important and intimate cultural act, allows us to show interest and concern for each other by building a common knowledge set, which, in turn, constructs stronger relationships through the discovery of shared experiences. Stories and institutional histories are two of the strongest foundations for WPA work. When we come together each year at the annual CWPA conference, we take time to learn from others' tales of victories and mistakes. For a young Black woman earning her doctorate at a top-tier university such as myself, the chance for renewal and inspiration at the conference has become a time for both reflection and resistance. Susan Miller's *Textual Carnivals* began to break the model of a single male-dominated narrative of WPA work with her discussion of historiography and composition programs, but Miller herself admits that she did not create a space for people of color in the book (566) and therefore, despite its brilliance, *Textual Carnivals* does not acknowledge the strengths of presenting numerous administrative histories that may include experiences from people of color.

Two popular narrative collections, Theresa Enos and Shane Borrowman's *The Promise and Perils of Writing Program Administration* and Diana George and Patricia Bizzell's *Kitchen Cooks, Plate Twirlers, and Troubadours: Writing Program Administrators Tell Their Stories* have the privilege of primacy to present a formal viewpoint for the writing program administrator experience. Like *Textual Carnivals*, both of these WPA narrative collections are also missing narratives from perspectives of WPAs of color. In *Kitchen Cooks, Plate Twirlers, and Troubadours*, the WPA is a disgruntled, fatherly graduate student and savior, but the program administrator in these identities is never a person of color. While the stories presented in these collections remain relevant, they do not fully encapsulate the complexities of identity, power, politics, and socialized histories for people of color in (and entering) administrative positions, especially at predominantly white institutions.

An historical examination of the HBCU Xavier University of Louisiana by Deany Cheramie reveals no evidence of a person of color administering the program in the first fifty years of the university's existence. Although there is evidence that an external reviewer recommended the development of a special fund for African American faculty to create a population of role models for Xavier students (159), there is no evidence that the university carried through with the recommendation. Even this historical look at HBCU writing program administration does not provide a view of WPA work from the perspective of a person of color. Rather, Cheramie's chapter reinforces the absence of stories that counter the unacknowledged view that WPA work does not belong to people of color. To address this false assumption of ownership, writing program administration scholarship and the CWPA organization must collect more narratives that link the individual experience of WPAs of color to the social collective and internal conversations that help validate the long-established use of storytelling in defining and decoding WPA work. Overall, the absence of people of color in the field's common histories, whether intentional or not, silently and systematically reaffirms the marginality of non-white, unprivileged narratives.

For emergent WPAs of color, the stories shared inside and outside the organization do not often portray our experiences. The few examples available are woeful tales of loss and critique. Collin Craig and Staci Perryman-Clark's "Troubling the Boundaries: (De)Constructing WPA Identities at the Intersections of Race and Gender" presents a heartbreaking narrative about racism and stereotyping as the experience for people of color at the CWPA annual conference. Their tale of exclusion and physical and emotional displacement dominates the field's existing narratives. While I applaud *WPA: Writing Program Administration*'s bravery and ability to publish such a polarizing account, I also ask myself, "Is that it? Is this the only narrative the journal has for people of color? Why this?"

Upon reading the article, I experienced every stage of grief: denial of the events; a feeling of isolation from my white male peers who could never relate; anger at the control structures in place that allowed the events to happen; bargaining with myself about studying WPA work in my doctoral program and my attendance at the conference; depression about my position as a person of color in WPA studies; and finally, acceptance that I could not change what happened to two young Black professionals like myself. I could investigate the culture fostering the professional development of young Black professionals and establish ways to share my own story as an emergent WPA of color with only a few other storytellers to move our experiences out of the margins. With the exception of Craig and Perryman-Clark, the presence of people of color in WPA studies is non-existant in 21st century scholarship. Such an absence and silence creates a clear and dangerous presentation of the work as uniquely gendered and racialized.

There must be more stories. The stories, much like the people who tell them, must be in hiding. We just have to find them.

There is precedence for this call to provide more narratives. Jacqueline Jones Royster and Jean Williams' seminal article "History in the Spaces Left" not only resists dominant narratives by offering a fully developed discussion of Blacks in composition studies, but also advocates in the closing statement that we need to "counter mythologies" (579) of composition scholarship in two ways: 1) by sharing that the presence of Blacks in composition studies is typically disregarded; and 2) by stating that there are ways that the experience of Blacks should change the histories of composition studies. In the National Census of Writing, only 7.1% of the 757 respondents to the question "With which racial groups and ethnic groups do you identify?" identified as belonging to a race or ethnicity outside of Caucasian at four-year institutions (writingcensus.swarthmore.edu), and a meager 2.4% of respondents identified as Black/African American specifically. Simply put, there are no narratives because—at least according to the census data—there are so few WPAs of color. I believe sharing the history of the few Blacks and other people of color in writing program administration would not only enhance the history of WPA studies but in turn, also alter its future for a generation of students who do not read themselves and their experiences in the pages of existing WPA narrative collections or hear their experiences at the annual conference. If we want to address the presence of whiteness within WPA work, then we cannot allow the harrowing experiences of Craig and Perryman-Clark be the only presentation of the people of color working tirelessly in administrative roles.

bell hooks affirms the importance of sharing narratives in *Thinking Feminist, Thinking Black*. hooks writes that longing to tell one's story and the process of telling is symbolically a gesture of longing to recover the past in such a way that one experiences both a sense of reunion and a sense of release (158). In addition to constructing spaces for reunion and release, hooks argues that failure to promote the construction of alternative narratives creates spaces where stories that do not fit the dominant model are "deemed illegitimate or unworthy of investigation" (hooks 110). I contend that seeking out and producing more narratives about WPAs of color takes up Royster and Williams' activism to resist the "official" narratives that create "symbolic systems of reality by which we draw the lines of the discipline and authenticate what is 'real' and not, significant enough to notice and not, or valuable and not" (580–81). To find the stories is to give them value. The stories would give people of color in WPA roles value and would, potentially, give stories to an emerging generation of writing program administrators.

In writing program administration, our stories inform our future. Every topic, every story, every victory, and every mistake presented in the many texts on WPA work in collections such as *Kitchen Cooks, Plate Twirlers, and Troubadours* and *Promise and Perils* inform us that WPAs are resilient accidental basement dwelling boat rocking fathers in an army of one. Our field is rich with scholars dedicated to change and advocacy. I believe the change is in the air. There are at least 7.1% of WPAs that can give voice to the silent narratives in *WPA: Writing Program Administration* and other publication venues. These stories deserve further investigation—for the next generation of WPAs and anyone who wished to understand the reward and rigor in WPA work as a person of color. I hope that someone takes up the challenge of presenting a new story time. I'll bring the milk and cookies.

Works Cited

Cheramie, Deany M. "Sifting through Fifty Years of Change: Writing Program Administration at an Historically Black University." Eds. Barbara E. L'Eplattenier and Lisa Mastrangelo. *Historical Studies of Writing Program Administration*. West Lafayette: Parlor P, 2004. 145–65. Print.

Craig, Collin Lamont, and Staci Maree Perryman-Clark. "Troubling the Boundaries: (De)Constructing WPA Identities at the Intersections of Race and Gender." *WPA: Writing Program Administration* 34.2 (2011): 37–58. Print.

Enos, Theresa and Shane Borrowman. *The Promise and Perils of Writing Program Administration*. West Lafayette: Parlor P, 2008. Print.

George, Diana, and Patricia Bizzell. *Kitchen Cooks, Plate Twirlers and Troubadours: Writing Program Administrators Tell Their Stories*. Portsmouth: Boynton/Cook: Heinemann, 1999. Print.

Gladstein, Jill, and Brandon Fralix. "Four-Year Institution Survey." *National Census on Writing. Swarthmore University*, 2015. Web. 24 November 2015.

hooks, bell. *Talking Back: Thinking Feminist, Thinking Black*. Cambridge: South End Press, 1989. Print.

Miller, Susan. *Textual Carnivals: The Politics of Composition*. Carbondale: Southern Illinois UP, 1991. Print.

Royster, Jacqueline Jones, and Jean C. Williams. "History in the Spaces Left: African American Presence and Narratives of Composition Studies." *College Composition and Communication* 50.4 (1999): 563–84. Print.

Sherri Craig is a doctoral candidate studying rhetoric and composition with specializations in writing program administration and professional writing at Purdue University, a Research 1 institution. Her research considers the intersections of mentoring, teacher preparation, and programmatic structures.

Troubling the Boundaries Revisited: Moving Towards Change as Things Stay the Same

Collin Lamont Craig and Staci M. Perryman-Clark

In our *WPA: Writing Program Administration* essay, "Troubling the Boundaries: (De)Constructing WPA Identities at the Intersections of Race and Gender," we examined "how looking at WPA work from both a gendered and racial perspective extends the implicative roles of identity politics in navigating administrative work within the context of university writing programs" (38). We wish to share how our experiences with race and gender identity politics in relation to WPA work have followed us in the work force. While these experiences indicate that the more things change, *the more they still stay the same*, they also demonstrate that, through rhetorical action, we can engage in the kinds of coalition building that bring awareness to inequities and racial microaggressions in strategic ways.

Staci Perryman-Clark Same Song, Different Verse: A Sista's Experience with Microagression and the Need for Allies

Microaggressions often reveal themselves when negotiating issues of power, authority, and *ethos*. These micoragressions require allies for faculty of color who are limited in power and authority when the WPA is both a person of color and untenured. As an untenured WPA, I was once asked to negotiate conflict between a white female TA and an African American male student. The TA claimed the student had been intimidating and disrespectful towards her during several meetings both inside and outside of class. While I observed disrespect and resistance in his attitude when he and the TA met with me about his work for her class, I had seen no evidence that he had been threatening or intimidating. The TA, nonetheless, requested that he be removed from her class because of her fears that a workable teacher/student relationship was no longer possible. My then department chair, a full professor and previous WPA, and I agreed to remove the student so the chair could work with him because we were less confident that she would grade him fairly since she was adamant that she never wanted to work with the student again. After reviewing and assessing samples of the student's work produced for the TA, we determined that it improved considerably over the course of working with my chair. The TA, however, sent an email request to assign the student's final grade because she assumed that the student was still enrolled in her course and was simply working one-on-one with the department chair outside of her class.

Because the TA's grade calculation differed from ours, the TA and her white, creative writing female graduate advisor (without any rhetoric and composition training) challenged our decision, even though the faculty advisor admitted that she found no fault in how I handled the situation when we spoke in a private conversation. After much discussion between us, the TA and faculty member microaggressively went behind our backs to our college dean and University Provost and requested that our jobs be terminated. However, the upper administration sided with the department chair and me and validated our assessment of the student's work.

Several issues of *ethos*/authority and power emerge. First, there is the assumption that a WPA and a faculty administrator, who had also been a WPA, must justify writing assessment decisions to an inexperienced, first-time TA with little background in composition pedagogy beyond a single composition methods course. While I believe that these can be learning moments for teaching assistants to cultivate best approaches to handling unfavorable tensions that occur on the job, these opportunities are undermined by the lack of regard and respect for my expertise as an administrator and assessment scholar of color.

Second, when WPAs of color do the work of running a writing program or protecting our students, our efforts also run the risks of being read only as agenda-driven race work, even when it is not. As a young, Black female administrator who has worked in writing programs that are predominately staffed with white faculty and TAs, the balancing act of advocating for racial and other marginalized minorities while ensuring a commitment to faculty and students across racial and gender lines can be a tricky one. Working from an intersecting racial and gender politic frequently positions us under a gaze that scrutinizes the ethical nature of the work that we do as Black women administrators. For example, after some discussion, the TA felt that neither my department chair nor I protected her from the male student's intimidation. The TA and her faculty advisor didn't understand why I as a female supposedly overlooked the student's lack of respect for women. So because I was Black, I questioned whether or not the TA and her faculty advisor assumed that I was playing favorites to the Black male student. Such accounts put us in positions to have to choose allegiances between our gender and race, as if they are not inextricably bound to each other.

Finally, untenured WPAs face the challenge of having to defend both the instructor/teaching assistant and student with fear of retaliation from faculty members. As a WPA building healthy mentoring relations with TAs, race can be a signifier that troubles the boundaries between racial paranoia and external attitudes of skeptical, white TAs who bring their issues with their students of color to my office. After I informed my department chair of the student's disrespect sans evidence of intimidation, my chair discussed the issue with the student who wept and apologized. Despite the student's apology, the TA and faculty advisor felt no remorse and still wanted to assign a lower grade, as if this would give them vindication for how they were treated. Despite my own reputation as a published and professionally recognized scholar in my field, the allusion of administrative agency or how "we" are seen as qualified directors becomes realized in our day-to-day interactions on the job. It is our allies, such as my departmental chair, who can be vital for navigating conflicts and survival as WPAs of color, especially microgressive behaviors that seek to undermine the *ethos*, power, and authority of WPAs of color.

Collin Lamont Craig—Building Allyship: Writing Program Administration as Collective Race Work

During the first year of my first tenure-track position, our Black female WPA left for another job. She left a card in my mailbox saying, "It's been great working with you in this short period that we shared in the program. I wish you well." She would later write about her experiences serving as our WPA in an article entitled "Teaching While Black: Witnessing and Countering Disciplinary Whiteness, Racial Violence, and Race-Management." She would recount the perils of navigating a predominately white institution as a Black female professor/administrator. She would expound on racial microaggressions she experienced from white faculty. These were colleagues whose offices were next to mine. So I figured I was next.

Patterns of racial violence in the form of institutional practices were all too familiar in my experiences as an assistant WPA while in graduate school. I had borne witness to and written about WPAs of color and the very few Black and Brown folks we saw at CWPA conferences. I had complained about the minimal scholarship that was written about intersectional microaggressions that faculty and WPAs experience (Craig and Perryman-Clark). I was aware of them. But I was also aware that my WPA's mentorship through these experiences was a critical component for my professional development as a junior tenure-track faculty of color.

After her swift exodus, I hit the ground running with my new job and buried myself in my work and service opportunities. I pursued a new research project to study Black college male literacies with a university mentoring program. Because the research project required me to miss faculty meetings, I notified the dean of the college and our program coordinator about this new research opportunity and was cleared to move forward with the project. But tensions grew from my administrator and my commitment to my program was called into question because of my absence at faculty meetings. He arranged a meeting with me, and I was chastised for these previously discussed and consented absences. He then questioned my overall progress as a junior faculty member. I was confused by this, considering that I was still actively participating in many program initiatives. I was on the committee that revised our program learning goals. I was mentoring graduate students teaching in the writing program. I co-coordinated our end of the year annual conference on student writing two years in a row and had recently published in a popular journal in my field. I found myself at odds and isolated while searching for advice to address my concerns about the experiences that I was having in my program.

In the aftermath of our WPA's exodus, fellow faculty members and I formed a teacher group out of a shared desire to keep race and multilingualism a central conversation for assessment and our pedagogical agendas. Our Race and Language group was a space for me to speak candidly as a marginalized faculty member in the midst of experiencing antagonistic racial encounters on [his] campus (Kynard). We wanted to think collectively about best practices for navigating campus racial microagressions. This group was comprised of both people of color and white colleagues interested in how race, language, and social justice could inform curriculum development and cross-disciplinary engagement. We theorized and imagined effective strategies for building allyship and thought through how racial allies might equally share in the stakes of those who represent the historically disenfranchised. We candidly spoke about what this said about white privilege. We collectively reflected on how white faculty must consider how much of their own privilege they are willing to forfeit for the cause of social justice. We also designated Perryman-Clark et al.'s *Students' Rights to Their Own Language: A Critical Sourcebook* as a framework for informing our conversations. That following summer we conducted a summer teacher workshop that organically evolved into a space for faculty-to-faculty mentoring. From those discussions we brainstormed ways that we could shape and shift conversations about why race matters for how we think about institutional whiteness as teachers and administrators.

That following semester a few of us from the Race and Language group enrolled our classes in the university's Learning Community (LC), a program that gives teachers opportunities to design out-of-class learning events for student engagement outside of the classroom. We themed our LC around race and social justice and organized cross-class movie viewings, museum trips, and spoken word workshops to discuss race and belonging at our university. We used university Speaker Series resources to invite a nationally recognized journalist from *The Nation* and prominent writer of the #blacklivesmatter movement to moderate a student panel on the value of college student activism. We forged collaborations with faculty from Education and English and gave workshops at the Center for Teaching and Learning (CTL) for campus-wide faculty that showcased approaches we used to responding to vernaculars in our classrooms. We believed that if we could also start a conversation about how teachers think about vernacular language practices across the disciplines, we were positioning them to think disciplinarily and institutionally about race, belonging, and culturally relevant teaching. This is the kind of rhetorical action that we believed could create meaningful ways for building efficacy in how we enacted programmatic and larger institutional conversations about whiteness, microaggressions, and racial inequities. This is the kind of rhetorical action that allowed us to imagine possibilities in the wake of experiencing how institutional whiteness and racism can marginalize or, at the very worst, intimidate or chase away faculty of color. We wanted to move from a place of reflection and critique to a place of bringing about programmatic and institutional change that felt real to us. We wanted to transform ways that we could bring about intra- and cross-disciplinary awareness in how race informs our curriculum, program administration and how we live in our bodies as faculty on predominately white campuses. In essence, this group became a safe space for allyship, where we could see the work that we did as faculty members as having a direct effect on the lives of our students and the professional lives of people of color. This was the sort of model I longed to see in other professional spaces.

Revisiting Troubling the Boundaries: Why Whiteness Studies Matters

As our narratives illustrate, racial and power dynamics continue to limit faculty of color's abilities to do WPA work. Yet we believe that while identifying opportunities to be change agents through cross-disciplinary coalition building, faculty-to-faculty mentoring, and program development is not always easy, it is possible. In "Troubling the Boundaries," we questioned the extent to which composition and CWPA are doing enough to address "how our disciplinary relations are also mediated by cultural difference" (53). We forward this discussion by further interrogating how whiteness functions institutionally, particularly in how whiteness maintains its power by defining (and denying) difference "on its own terms and to its own advantage" (Barnett 10). To CWPA we ask: How do we employ discursive practices through conference themes, scholarship, and missions that variably or invariably position whiteness as a power structure that denies cultural differences that exist among all of its members and constituents? We raise this critical question because we wonder to what extent CWPA becomes implicit and explicit in using whiteness as a discourse that reinforces its own privilege by denying and ignoring cultural difference in relation to white privilege.

Revisiting our recommendations in "Troubling the Boundaries," then, suggests CWPA members and constituents begin to not only address cultural difference (53); it also suggests that we transform difference into action by being stronger allies and support systems for junior faculty/WPAs, and WPAs of color, especially as they navigate racial microagressions that may potentially go unchecked and unnoticed. With regard to current initiatives, we applaud CWPA's Mentor Project and the following dialogue as a step in the right direction. We also acknowledge that WPA faculty of color still need stronger advocacy and broader institutional (white) allies in building administrative support. As we consider the ways in which we might use our understandings of whiteness studies to work for a greater, collective good, we propose CWPA as the next intellectual space that engages whiteness as a call to action.

We propose white allies to work toward a collective good as they support faculty and WPAs of color.

Works Cited

Barnett, Timothy. "Reading 'Whiteness' in English Studies." *College English* (2000): 9–37. Print.

Craig, Collin Lamont, and Staci Maree Perryman-Clark. "Troubling the Boundaries: (De) Constructing WPA Identities at the Intersections of Race and Gender." *WPA: Writing Program Administration* 34.2 (2011): 37–58. Print.

Kynard, Carmen. "Teaching While Black: Witnessing Disciplinary Whiteness, Racial Violence, and Race-Management." *Literacy in Composition Studies* 3.1 (2015): 1–20. Print.

Perryman-Clark, Staci, David E. Kirkland, and Austin Jackson. *Students' Rights to Their Own Language: A Critical Sourcebook*. New York: Bedford/St. Martin, 2014. Print.

Staci M. Perryman-Clark is associate professor of English and Director of First-Year Writing at Western Michigan University, a public research university. She is the author of Afrocentric Teacher-Research: Rethinking Appropriateness and Inclusion *(Peter Lang, 2013), and the co-editor of* Students' Right to Their Own Language: A Critical Sourcebook *(2014). She is the 2015 recipient of the Western Michigan University College of Arts and Sciences Award for Research and Creative Activity. She has published widely in rhetoric and composition studies.*

Collin Lamont Craig is an assistant professor at St. John's University, a private, Roman Catholic, co-educational university. His research explores Black college male place-making practices as rhetorical production. He specifically explores these practices within university-sponsored affinity groups such as the Black Male Initiative. His book project investigates how Black and Latino college males use a range of literacies for identity formation, cultural production, and place making at predominately white institutions. His interests in cultural rhetoric and 21st century literacy education inform his teaching and commitment to equity and access to higher education.

Notes on Race in Transnational Writing Program Administration

Amy A. Zenger

The global turn in Rhetoric and Composition is evidenced by international and transnational research initiatives, international conferences, transnational writing programs, and cross border teaching collaborations and consultancies (see Thaiss et al; Donahue). Writing programs outside of the US with links to Rhetoric and Composition in the US represent one dimension of an expanded picture of writing studies. David S. Martins's *Transnational Writing Program Administration* highlights the diversity of forms that such programs may take. It is not uncommon for North American universities to open international branch campuses, many of which include writing instruction or writing programs such as required undergraduate courses, WAC/WID, and writing centers. Educational exchanges can also link classrooms or programs in two or more sites across international borders. Many independent universities outside of the US also claim adherence to an American liberal arts tradition, including having composition programs, a commitment typically flagged in the name of the institution (and often with some informal connection to specific American institutions), as in the American University in Cairo, American University of Bulgaria, and so on. While the global landscape of writing studies and writing program administration is much more complex than this, here I would like to focus specifically on these US-linked or -inspired transnational programs.[1] I write from the perspective of a compositionist trained in the US who is teaching and administering programs in a liberal arts university in Lebanon in which English is the language of instruction for all undergraduate and graduate courses, except for Arabic courses and occasional teaching of other languages, such as Chinese or Turkish.

Many contributors to *Transnational Writing Program Administration* document challenges to familiar approaches and expectations experienced by teachers and administrators trained in institutions in North America and working in non-Western contexts. Defamiliarization can offer insights into previously unquestioned assumptions about writing and writing instruction and the hard-to-see ideological forces at work in everyday decision-making and administrative practices, as Bruce Horner notes in an afterword to the collection. One ideological factor not taken up directly in these essays, however, is race. The relevance of studies emerging in the US context may not be readily apparent for other contexts since race is articulated differently from one location to the next and from one historical period to the next. As David Lloyd observes, "the analysis of the formation of these categories [race, gender, and class, among others] in relation to the subject of ideology ultimately requires an unrelenting specificity" and grounding in material histories (267). As a discipline, Rhetoric and Composition has historically been closely aligned with US national boundaries; when Rhet/Comp pedagogies, administrative structures, and learning goals and outcomes are introduced into different national contexts, they acquire added layers of complexity, not only because they may be difficult to enact for material or other reasons, but also because they then become active as one part of a more complex educational landscape with its own histories and social categories.

One way to set the stage for thinking about how race plays out in writing program administration in different locations is to take global relations of power into account explicitly. My comments here are framed by the work of Charles Mills, whose theory of race attempts to "account for the way things are and how they came to be that way" on a global scale (10). In *The Racial Contract*, Mills argues that Western ideals of social and political organization, the state, and judicial systems, as expressed in social contract theory, are constituted by a pre-political system of race that already demarcates the inequalities in how whites and non-whites may participate. His theory is important because it encompasses both normed/white and un-normed/non-white individuals and phenomena: "race is in no way an 'afterthought,' a 'deviation' from ostensibly raceless Western ideals" (14). It becomes our obligation to look at all programs in terms of racial formations, not just those that have primarily non-white populations or that are situated outside of the West.

According to Mills, race as a system "norms (and races) space" on different scales:

> The norming of space is partially done in terms of the *racing* of space, the depiction of space as dominated by individuals . . . of a certain race. At the same time, the norming of the individual is partially achieved by *spacing* it, that is, representing it as imprinted with the characteristics of a certain space. (41–42; emphasis original)

Racialized spatial terms structure the experiences and motivations for engaging in composition work differently for different actors involved, depending on what they desire to have or are allowed to obtain from the interaction. People have unequal rights to international mobility, depending on their citizenship or identification. For North American or European citizens, the right to travel to see the world and to work in different locations is often taken for granted, if sometimes limited by fears for personal safety. For Western academics, taking a position abroad is typically a short-term commitment (Badry and Willoughby 167); for some it can be "career suicide" (Healey 66) while for others it represents the experience needed to obtain a permanent position in the West or simply an adventure. For citizens of other nationalities or identity groups, however, the right to travel for work, to study, to attend conferences, or to travel for pleasure is often much more restricted. Even when visas are available, the process of obtaining them can be time-consuming and expensive and still may not guarantee permission to travel. Hiring decisions also mean choosing whether to hire internationally or locally. In a different sense, doctoral programs in Rhetoric and Composition are still located in the West; diversifying the transnational WPA position may therefore be difficult without broadening the search to other disciplines. Conventional administrative structures may also need to be modified, if, as has been the case at my institution, program continuity, cultural knowledge, institutional memory, and local experience inhere in the pool of instructors, while disciplinary expertise and the power to engage in university governance inhere in a rotating population of professorial rank hires.

Inequalities also structure knowledge production and access to knowledge centered in research centers, publications, and universities. Researchers in this region may be committed to making contributions locally but compelled for professional reasons to publish internationally. Acutely aware of the need to frame their research carefully, they consider who will benefit from it, where it will be published, and in which language it will appear—a local language, such as Arabic, or the universal language of scholarship, English (Riazi). Regional areas, defined in such formations as Southeast Asia and the Middle East, can shape research but also reflect the perspectives of Western academics that are not necessarily the perceptions of inhabitants within those regions (Anderson). As Mignolo cautions: "Regions are not objects of study or mines from which to extract 'cultural resources' to be processed in the industrial epistemic centers of Western Europe and the United States" (269). Compositionists working outside of the center will almost certainly share their work in Western venues and would also do well to be critical about how they engage in the field and how they participate in the creation and circulation of knowledge in a system that is heavily weighted towards the West.

Mills also argues that the Racial Contract is "historically locatable in the series of events marking the creation of the modern world by European colonialism and the voyages of 'discovery'" (20). Historical study is a powerful way to demystify assumptions about common practices and methods in teaching and administration. I can identify two areas that cry out for historicization in the context where I work: 1) the adoption of English as the medium of instruction (circa 1880 at my university) and 2) the common use of particular genres in the teaching of writing. Horner and Trimbur traced the establishment of monolingualist ideologies and practices in the US by studying how American universities shifted away from classical languages and adopted modern languages; I suggest that the shift to monolingualism in the US also specifically championed English in a choice driven by racialized language ideologies (Zenger). While several scholars have noted that students in transnational contexts often struggle to read critically and to produce certain genres successfully, research to address this question has focused primarily on adapting methods to support the academic success of students without questioning the genres students are being asked to perform. I am interested in studying the historical formation of genres that were shaped in the early days of composition when university education defined the cultivated man as one who exhibited independent thinking and the navigation of free choice, individualism, and objective detachment, qualities frequently defined against representations of others, including slaves, former slaves, or students in madrassas.

Finally, Mills argues that the Racial Contract is epistemological: "*White misunderstanding, misrepresentation, evasion, and self-deception on matters related to race* are among the most pervasive mental phenomena of the past few hundred years" (19). If defamiliarization can provoke insights about our everyday practices, as Horner suggests, white epistemology is a powerful force that works against new insights. Other conditions can also stand in the way: If faculty members are employed on shorter contracts or are not supported by tenure, they may not be in a position to make significant changes. If they are working outside of their own culture, they may also lack historical and linguistic knowledge needed to have a material understanding of the local context. Challenging whiteness in writing program administration anywhere is necessarily a project of difficult analysis, but it cannot only be about analysis; it must aim to change how we understand and carry out everyday actions in our work. We ought to be willing to hold our knowledge "in parentheses" (to use Walter Mignolo's expression) as we act in the world to decide goals and outcomes for programs and courses, assessment and placement practices, texts to adopt, and pedagogical approaches. We have traditions of anti-racist thinking and activism in both American traditions and other traditions to which we can turn. The perceived need for English and composition instruction continues to drive the establishment of transnational programs, and we can see these as opportunities to contribute to research outside of the West and to continue to question methodologies and practices both outside and inside American borders. These necessarily brief notes are intended to contribute to further discussion.

Notes

1. Although I use the term *transnational* to describe programs with administrative and intellectual ties that cross national borders, I am not persuaded that the programs are in fact all characterized by a critical stance in relation to globalization, the sense that led to the coining of the term by Aihwa Ong. This can be a discussion for another time, however.

Works Cited

Anderson, Benedict. "Introduction." *The Spectre of Comparisons: Nationalism, Southeast Asia, and the World*. London: Verso, 1998. 1–28. Print.

Badry, Fatima, and John Willoughby. *Higher Education Revolutions in the Gulf: Globalization and Institutional Viability*. New York: Routledge. 2004. Print.

Donahue, Christiane. "'Internationalization' and Composition Studies: Reorienting the Discourse." *College Composition and Communication* 61.2 (2009): 212–43. Print.

Healey, Nigel M. "The Challenges of Leading an International Branch Campus: The 'Lived Experience' of In-Country Senior Managers." *Journal of Studies in International Education* 20.1 (2016): 61–78. Web.

Horner, Bruce. "Afterword: Transnational Writing Program Administration." *Transnational Writing Program Administration.* Ed. David S. Martins. Logan: Utah State UP, 2015.

Horner, Bruce, and John Trimbur. "English Only and US College Composition." *College Composition and Communication* 53.4 (2002): 594–630. Web. 14 Feb. 2015. Print.

Lloyd, David. "Race Under Representation." *Culture/Contexture: Explorations in Anthropology and Literary Studies.* Ed. E. Valentine Daniel and Jeffrey M. Peck. Berkeley: U of California P, 1996. Print.

Martins, David S., ed. *Transnational Writing Program Administration.* Logan: Utah State UP, 2015. Print.

Mignolo, Walter. "The Point of Nonreturn: The Reemergence of the Disavowed." *Comparative Studies of South Asia, Africa, and the Middle East.* 33.3 (2013): 268–71. Web. 6 April 2016.

Riazi, Mehdi. "Producing Scholarly Texts: Writing in English in a Politically Stigmatized Country." *International Advances in Writing Research: Cultures, Places, Measures.* Ed. Charles Bazerman, Chris Dean, Jessica Early, Karen Lunsford, Suzie Null, Paul Rogers, and Amanda Stansell. Fort Collins: WAC Clearinghouse and Parlor P, 2012. 449–66. Print.

Thaiss, Chris, Gerd Bräuer, Paula Carlino, Lisa Ganobscik-Williams, and Aparna Sinha, eds. *Writing Programs Worldwide: Profiles of Academic Writing in Many Places.* Fort Collins: WAC Clearinghouse and Parlor P, 2012. Web. 1 Sept. 2014.

Zenger, Amy. "Composition and 'Our English': Performing the Mother Tongue in the Daily Themes for English 12 at Harvard, 1886–87." *Rhetoric Review.* 23.4 (2004): 332–49. Print.

Amy A. Zenger is associate professor of English at the American University of Beirut, a private, non-profit, teaching-centered research university in Beirut, Lebanon. The university adheres to an American model of liberal arts education and is committed to serving the peoples of the Middle East and beyond. She directed the university Writing Center at AUB for several years. Her most recent book, co-edited with Bronwyn Williams, is New Media Literacies and Participatory Popular Culture across Borders *(Routledge, 2012).*

Sustaining Balance: Writing Program Administration and the Mentorship of Minority College Students

Regina McManigell Grijalva

Higher education is rapidly shifting; this shift parallels the changing demographics in the US's population. The once dominant non-Hispanic white social group in the US is dwindling while the number of people from minoritized groups continues to grow. According to 2014 US Census Bureau data, the general population of adults in the US in 2014 was made up of about 62.1% non-Hispanic whites and 37.9% people from all other minoritized groups ("Quick Facts"). However, the population under the age of five in 2014 was comprised of about 49.5% non-Hispanic whites and 50.5% people from minoritized groups (Yen). However, the ethnicity and culture of teachers and professors are not changing as quickly. The number of professionals in 2014 with a PhD was around .18% of the total population, and only .09% of the US population with a PhD was from a minoritized group ("Educational Attainment"). The diversity of professors in higher education cannot match or keep up with the growing diversity of the students that will soon become their students.

Like traditional—e.g., non-Hispanic white—students, diverse students need mentors they can identify with. For students from minoritized groups, having mentors with strong cultural competence might mean the difference between staying in school to graduate or leaving without a degree. In fact, although all minoritized students are at risk for dropping out of college, minoritized males are the most likely to not make it to college, and of those who do, they are the most likely to leave without a degree (Harper). One reason that diverse faculty tend to be more culturally competent is their own personal understanding of and experience with diversity. This is supported by the research of Milem and Umbach which suggested that female faculty and faculty from diverse groups were more likely to employ learner-centered or interactive teaching/learning techniques in the classroom and were more likely to be aware of research in/of race, ethnicity, and gender. As members of minoritized groups themselves, diverse faculty members have had to navigate through a system with few people like themselves. For diverse faculty members, cultural competence, as a skill of adapting to various cultural communication patterns and norms, is often born out of the necessity to survive in a world of difference.

Even with a small number of minority professors, cultural competence is still one of the greatest strengths that the US maintains in a global economy. Damon Williams underscores this idea saying that the global economy "highlights the particular opportunity, and competitive advantage, that the US still holds in the world" (2). But it is not enough that we have a diverse nation. We must ensure that our diverse young students have a chance at higher education, or many will continue to have limited opportunities at earning a college degree. Research points to the "link between low levels of educational attainment and high risks of incarceration . . . of particular subgroups of the population" (Ewart and Wildhagen 3–4). In fact, Blacks, Hispanics, and Native Americans are less likely to graduate from high school or even attend college—let alone graduate from college—and are more likely to be incarcerated than their non-Hispanic white counterparts (see Alexander; Cassleman; Ewart and Wildhagen; US Dept. of Justice "Special Report" and *Sourcebook*; Wolf Harlow). Armed with this knowledge about the exigence of educating and retaining college students of color, my approach to battling these depressing facts included creating a community of concern with colleagues across my university campus.

As a multicultural scholar from a Latina and Native background, creating community and building relationships is a cultural asset of mine. However, creating community can take time, and, as an untenured WPA on the tenure track, my job requirements are demanding. My desire to mentor students (and faculty) of color while continuing to fulfill my assigned duties creates the potential for burnout, so I must be wise about how I balance these activities.

My university is a small liberal arts college with a student population comprised of about 70% non-Hispanic whites and 30% minority students, a ratio similar to the US adult population with just a few percentage points under in minority students and a few over in the dominant group's number (as noted above, the total US population ratio was roughly 62:38 in 2014). The faculty population at my campus is comprised of about 90% non-Hispanic whites and 10% faculty from minoritized groups. Additionally, we have a scholarship program designated specifically for students from underrepresented groups. I work directly with these diverse student-scholars beyond my program and department, and this work has led me to foster relationships with like-minded people across the campus. This common interest in students from underrepresented groups brought faculty from four disciplines (education, English, mathematics, and religion) together with administrators and staff members from Student Affairs to do programmatic planning that enhances the scholarship program for such students. Though the scholarship program had been in place for seven years by the time I came to the campus, it had no previous programming that involved faculty members before this group began collaborating.

We started with an informal discussion of whether a summer bridging program would better meet students' needs. We formed a Faculty Learning Community, a group of people including but not limited to faculty interested in studying ways to impact teaching and learning, supported by our Center for Excellence in Teaching and Learning (CETL). CETL provided a meeting space and funding for study materials, meals, or conference travel. We studied diversity together, often discussing our findings over a meal. We looked over admissions data and determined that the students who could benefit most from a summer program would be incoming scholars who identified with an underrepresented group. However, even setting funds aside for minoritized or underrepresented students can be problematic. In collaborating with these colleagues and studying diversity in higher education, I discovered (what my Student Affairs colleagues already knew) how controversial just verbalizing the desire to help minority students can be. For example, in 1978, the Supreme Court ruled in *University of California v. Bakke,* upholding the use of race and ethnicity in admissions, but in Texas in 1996 in *Hopwood v. Texas,* the Court of Appeals denied the use of race and ethnicity. Two more current Supreme Court cases, *Gratz v. Bollinger* in 2003 and *Fisher v. University of Texas at Austin* in 2013, affirmed the use of race and ethnicity. Studying diversity in higher education and working with this group of colleagues opened my eyes to how controversial race and ethnicity can be.

After some research together, we decided to implement a summer bridging program called Mind the Gap for students who were awarded the scholarships based on identification with underrepresented groups. Historically, the other scholarship criterion was leadership in the community. For the summer program, we set up service opportunities for students at several nearby nonprofits; a choice of two required general education classes (English Composition, Study Skills, Algebra, or World Religions); an hour of study time with professors for every hour of instruction; and co-curricular activities such as ropes courses, and visits to cultural centers and performing and/or fine art shows. We gathered data before, during, and after the summer program, as well as at the end of each subsequent year through surveys, questionnaires, and focus groups. The scholarship program boasts a 94% retention rate compared to the overall 86% retention rate for the larger university campus.

We have gathered plenty of data over the years to demonstrate the success of our efforts as reflected by students' opinions of their learning and service and by institutional data on the students collected by our institutional research office. Everyone involved in the programmatic planning of Mind the Gap came into direct contact with the scholars. There were eight of us in the beginning: half from the academic side and half from the Student Affairs side of the university. The number of incoming student-scholars over four years averaged 29 per year, but mentoring this group of students has seemed less time-consuming than one might imagine, since there have been a large number of mentors for these student-scholars. In addition, there are upperclassmen mentors, whom we continue to support. Many of the student-scholars take on roles such as sophomore advisors or junior/senior mentors and are available to help mentor the first-year scholars. This kind of bottom-up and top-down mentoring makes my professional life as a WPA sustainable.

However, though I have forged strong relationships across campus with many fantastic colleagues of diversity, many have found other jobs with either higher pay or better positions or both. Since there are fewer of us on board with the scholarship program now, we have restructured it so it continues to be sustainable work. We still have students taking General Education classes and doing community service projects together, but our number as well as the number of student-scholars has dwindled. There are three mentors today (instead of the original eight), one faculty member and two administrators from Student Affairs and only twenty incoming student-scholars this year. Though the numbers have decreased, the mentors involved still believe we are making a difference in the lives of minoritized students and are hopeful that the number of student-scholars and mentors will increase in the near future.

Works Cited

Alexander, Michelle. *The New Jim Crow: Mass Incarceration in the Age of Colorblindness*. New York: New Press, 2012. Print.

Cassleman, Ben. "Race Gap Narrows in College Enrollment, But Not in Graduation." *FiveThirtyEight*. 30 Apr. 2014.Web. 10 July 2015.

Ewart, Stephanie, and Tara Wildhagen. "Educational Characteristics of Prisoners: Data from the *ACS*." Paper presented at the Population Association of America Annual Meeting, Washington DC, March 31-April 2, 2011. Print.

Gratz v. Bollinger. 539 US 244. Supreme Court of the US. 2003. Web. 16 July 2015.

Fisher v. University of Texas at Austin. 133 S. Ct. 2411. Supreme Court of the US. 2013. Web. 16 July 2015.

"Educational Attainment." *United States Census Bureau*. 2014. Web. 24 Nov. 2014.

Harper, Shaun. "Five Things Student Affairs Administrators Can Do to Improve Student Success among College Men of Color." Issue Brief. NASPA Research and Policy Institute. Mar. 2013. Web. 9 July 2015.

Hopwood v. State of Texas. 236 F. 3d 256. US Court of Appeals, Fifth Circuit. 2000. Web 16 July 2015.

Milem, Jeffrey F., and Paul D. Umbach. "Understanding the Difference Diversity Makes: Faculty Beliefs, Attitudes, and Behaviors." *Creating Inclusive Campus Environments: For Cross-Cultural Learning and Student Engagement*. Ed. Shaun R. Harper. Washington, DC: NASPA, 2008. Print.

"Quick Facts." *United States Census Bureau*. 2014. Web. 24 Nov. 2014.

United States Bureau of Justice. *Sourcebook of Criminal Justice* Statistics Online. Office of Justice Programs, Bureau of Justice Statistics. 2012. Print.

University of California Regents v. Bakke. 438 US 265. Supreme Court of the United States. 1978. Web. 16 July 2015.

Williams, Damon A. *Strategic Diversity Leadership: Activating Change and Transformation in Higher Education.* Sterling: Stylus Publishing, 2013. Print.

Wolf Harlow, Caroline. "Educational and Correctional Populations." United States Bureau of Justice. Office of Justice Programs, Bureau of Justice Statistics. 2003. Print.

Yen, Hope. "Census: White Majority in U.S. Gone by 2043." *NBC News.* 13 June 2013, US News Ed. Web. 9 July 2015.

Regina McManigell Grijalva is Associate Professor of English and Director of Composition at Oklahoma City University, a small liberal arts college nestled in the urban center of Oklahoma City and affiliated with the United Methodist Church. With her colleague, Amrita Sen, McManigell Grijalva directs the Global and Transnational Migrations Digital Archives Project. Much of her research focuses on pedagogy, learning, and assessment in higher education and the ways they interact with class, race, ethnicity, and/or gender. Her recent longitudinal study of high school to college learning will appear in the forthcoming collection, Critical Transitions: A Question of Transfer.

WPA and the New Civil Rights Movement

Genevieve García de Müeller

If writing program administrators are to create an inclusive and diverse environment, then WPA work must be relocated in an activist context aimed at advocating for the rights of students of color. As a way to model how WPAs might work in an activist context, in this article, I look at one student-led civil rights movement. Migrant student activists, particularly DREAMers, have generated pragmatic ways to advocate for migrant rights by appropriating the genres and rhetorical moves of the dominant institution with non-assimilationist methods (García de Müeller). The migrant activist WPA seeks to not only engage with the ethnolinguistically diverse migrant population and work towards transference of skills but also to fully accept the fact that migrant activists are adept at appropriating the dominant discourse, manipulating it, and shaping it to their needs. The migrant activist WPA seeks not to use these transference of skills as a mode of assimilation into the academy but as a path for migrant undocumented students to change academic discourse and to combat racist structures on and beyond the university.

THE NEW MIGRANT CIVIL RIGHTS MOVEMENT

This new migrant civil rights movement is embedded in the notion that citizenship is a way for a nation state to uphold inequality. Immigration policy in the US is used to "perpetuate a privileged lifestyle at the expense of foreigners" and so is often written favoring economic benefit over social well-being (Isbister 85). Migrant undocumented students not only have to fight against immigration structures invested in economic disparity and marginalization, they also have to carve out spaces in the university that honor their ethnolinguistic background in the hope of instituting change. WPAs may provide paths for migrant undocumented students to create such spaces.

In his call for the CWPA to self-reflect on diversity, Jonathan Alexander writes

> Appreciation isn't analysis. Tolerance isn't critique. Adding a reading by a lesbian or a black man or an Asian woman might be nice, but doing so doesn't examine the very real discourses that might tempt one to make such an inclusion in the first place, much less understand how doing so fails to address substantively the discourses of bigotry and "othering" that circulate so widely in our culture. It fails in so many ways to address the lived and felt experience of walking around, knowing that others think of you as less than. (166)

Including texts by diverse authors is a political move but not a big enough one. Alexander is right in saying that "appreciation isn't analysis," but the power of representation and precedence for diverse scholars in the classroom—as authors of texts and as instructors— cannot be denied. Representation is vitally important but so is a critical analysis of how and why academia is embedded in white dominant discourses. Many WPAs of color have worked to add diversity to the canon, but rarely do writing programs have systems that value the diverse logics and rhetorics students employ or the diverse rhetorical and discursive skills students already possess. Migrant activist work intersected with WPA work is a fruitful way to include various ways of knowing and strategies of appropriating dominant discourse while avoiding assimilation.

The task to interrogate WPA work through the lens of race and ethnicity is daunting and requires more than a look at the lack of representation of minoritized groups, although that is an important task as well. If the values and principles of WPA work change, then the assessment strategies, the outcomes, and the definitions of academic discourse must too. After their racist experiences at a CWPA conference that included someone calling them the "WPA's bitches" and someone else denying Craig entrance into dinner due to his Black maleness, Craig and Perryman-Clark wrote

> as folks of color who have grown too accustomed to reactive rather that proactive responses to racial insensitivity, we wonder if WPA as a sub-discipline in composition and rhetoric is doing enough in addressing issues that reveal how our disciplinary relations are also mediated by cultural differences. (53)

Besides looking at the programs WPAs institute and the values WPAs have in regards to language use, Standard American English, academic writing, and ethnolinguistic diversity, WPAs must also consider the kinds of responses they have when faced with problems concerning diversity.

Reactive strategies to issues of diversity and racism might deal with how to navigate around the issue by avoiding the discussion of diversity and opting for a rhetoric centered on the universality of problems. In a sense, ignoring the race problem by ignoring differing race experiences allows us to homogenize WPA work. These reactions happen too often and don't account for the fact that difference is a very crucial and integral part of how students navigate the university and therefore cannot be ignored:

> it is crucial that those in rhetorical and cultural studies who are concerned with interrogating the construction of social identity and formation of structures of social inequality continue to focus on difference precisely because humans have defined and continue to define one another by their differences. (West 32)

Ignoring difference leads to colorblind racist attempts at pretending race does not matter when, even though race is socially constructed in human interactions, it is a very real concept. Because of the gatekeeping aspect of composition and the privileging of the dominant discourses, writing programs are often a place where race matters a great deal and the stakes are high. Ruth Spack argues

> [T]eachers are not abstract; they are women or men of particular races, classes, ages, abilities, and so on. The teacher will be seen and heard by students not as an abstraction, but as a particular person with a certain defined history and relationship to the world. (11)

In many ways, the students are affected by the identity of the writing instructor, the writing program, and the values brought into the classroom.

As Craig writes, "I became interested in WPA work because I believed that a writing program was more than just a place that housed required first-year writing courses. For me, the WPA could be a conscious community builder" (Craig and Perryman-Clark 46). Out of necessity and support, WPAs of color are particularly adept at looking at the possibilities for community building within academia and within writing programs.

One example of this is the recent formation of the CWPA People of Color Caucus as a systematic way to increase representation of academics of color in the CWPA and as a means to intersect race and WPA work in a public platform. Looking at WPA work in relation to race and ethnicity produces the kind of interconnectedness Craig is calling for when he writes, "situating intersectionality in WPA scholarship builds on existing conversations that acknowledge how WPAs learn how to navigate and negotiate their multiple identities for institutional agency and program building" (Craig and Perryman-Clark 39). WPAs of color navigate their identities in their dual roles as writing program admins and community builders bridging campus and community in meaningful ways. These community bridging efforts are vital spaces to explore how to create programmatic shifts that honor linguistic diversity.

Writing Across Communities at the HSI University of New Mexico works to create "literacy education programs that foreground the values of community and sustainability" in order to "enhance students' initiation into a complex ecology of human relationships" (Hall Kells 89). Writing Across Communities is focused on providing "those who have been historically under served, with the tools they need as citizens in the making—to navigate and negotiate the varied linguistic and cultural circumstances they face in their everyday lives both on and off campus" (Guerra 73). In many ways, Writing Across Communities is entrenched in transcultural repositioning or "a notion grounded in the idea that members of historically excluded groups are in a position to cultivate adaptive strategies that help them move across cultural boundaries by negotiating new and different contexts and communicative conventions" (Guerra 299). These kinds of efforts—mentoring networks for scholars of color, programs built to support students of color, and systematic program changes based on theories respecting linguistic diversity—are ways to increase diversity in higher education while also resisting assimilationist deficit-based models. Migrant activist writing is another example of transcultural repositioning. By using genres of the dominant discourse, "DREAMers shift into the public realm by synthesizing and interpreting legislative documents, combatting racist ideologies, and disseminating knowledge to a community of linguistically and socially diverse undocumented students" (García de Müeller). For example, to combat criminalizing and xenophobic rhetoric in US immigration policy, such as the Development Relief and Education of Alien Minors Act, more commonly known as the DREAM act, DREAMers use personal narratives that depict migrants of "good moral character" (García de Müeller). By utilizing migrant activist genres, students develop their own writing identities as emerging scholars by considering how language, power, and identity influence how writers are shaped by and shape communities and legislation. The migrant rights movement uses pragmatic strategies to affect and change the discourse surrounding US immigration policy. When the US blocks public assembly, DREAMers assemble on the Internet. They control the visuals, control the rhetoric, and interpret and provide quick and easy resources. When the US legislative texts create a criminal profile, DREAMers combat it with personal stories of triumph. Migrant activists show audience awareness and push immigrants into the public. When the US writes impossible legislation, DREAMers re-write it; they make new conditions, create new provisions, and make compromises that still adhere to a central goal. Migrant student activists have created community models and activist genres that align with campus initiatives and provide ways for WPAs to situate their work in an activist context while negotiating their identity in institutions that uphold predominantly white discourses. Instituting a Writing Across Communities program using migrant activist models and writing practices is one way WPAs can reframe WPA work.

This negotiation of identity needs to resist a compromise of values. Thomas West writes

> Understanding negotiation as strict compromise or as navigation, as the smoothing over of tensions rather than the exploration and interrogation of them, needs to be supplemented and/or replaced by a model of critical negotiation, a strategy that highlights not only the (re)formation of meaning and subjectivity during moments of social and political interaction but one that also takes into account the role and effect of emotion during these moments. (15)

The migrant activist student uses language for powerful political ends, enters the academy, and changes it. The migrant activist student sees their "self as situated within a discipline and within the world, confronting racism head on as well as other situations that distance women, the poor, and others from the dominant discourse and its racialized and gendered assumptions" (Villanueva 172). The migrant undocumented student-run movement is beyond multiculturalism and its aesthetic, surface-level empty acts of "tolerance" and "appreciation" of various cultures and identities. It works against a deficit model by showing that not only do migrant activist writing practices intentionally and critically appropriate the dominant discourse, they also work against assimilation.

Ultimately, the migrant activist WPA works at the intersections of migrant activist work and student of color transfer into the university while acknowledging and valuing the ways in which migrant students reposition their linguistic skills into an academic setting while also shifting the linguistic landscape of the university. These changes will cause necessary self-interrogation in WPA work that focuses on the intersections between administering writing programs and race, ethnicity, linguistic diversity, and citizenship. The migrant activist is at the center of this interrogation and may provide ways in which the WPA can implement diversity goals without subjugating ethnolinguistically diverse students to an assimilationist agenda.

Works Cited

Alexander, Jonathan. "Literacy and Diversity: A Provocation." *WPA: Writing Program Administration* 33.1–2 (Fall/Winter 2009). 164–68. Print.

Craig, Collin Lamont, and Staci Maree Perryman-Clark. "Troubling the Boundaries: (De)Constructing WPA Identities at the Intersections of Race and Gender" *WPA: Writing Program Administration* 34.2 (2011): 37–58. Print.

García de Müeller, Genevieve. "Digital DREAMS: The Rhetorical Power of Online Resources for DREAM Act Activists." *Linguistically Diverse Immigrant and Resident Writers*. Ed. Todd Ruecker and Christina Ortmeier-Hooper. Forthcoming, 2016. Print.

Guerra, Juan. "Cultivating Transcultural Citizenship: A Writing Across Communities Model." *Language Arts* 85.4 (2008). 296–304. Print.

Hall Kells, Michelle. "Writing Across Communities: Diversity, Deliberation, and the Discursive Possibilities of WAC." *Reflections* 6.1 (Spring 2007): 87–108. Print.

Isbister, John. "Are Immigration Controls Ethical?" *Immigration: A Civil Rights Issue for the Americas*. Ed. Suzanne Jonas. New York: Rowman and Littlefield Publishers, 1998. Print.

Spack, Ruth. "The (In)Visibility of the Person(al) in Academe." *College English* 59.1 (1997): 9–31. Print.

Villanueva, Victor. "On the Rhetoric and Precedents of Racism." *College Composition and Communication* 50.4 (1999): 645–61. Print.

West, Thomas. "The Racist Other." Special Issue: Race, Class, Writing. *JAC* 17.2 (1997): 215–26. Print.

Genevieve García de Müeller is an Assistant Professor at the University of Texas Rio Grande Valley, a large, majority-minority Hispanic serving institute on the border. Her work focuses on civil rights rhetoric and multilingual composition. She is currently on the Council for Writing Program Administrators Diversity Committee and is the founder and chair of the CWPA People of Color Caucus. Her study on migrant activist genres titled, "Digital DREAMS: The Rhetorical Power of Online Resources for DREAM Act Activists" will be published in the edited collection Linguistically Diverse Immigrant and Resident Writers *(Routledge, forthcoming).*

The Yardstick of Whiteness in Composition Textbooks

Cedric D. Burrows

During a debate at Oxford University, Malcolm X contended "When you're in a position of power for a long time, you get used to using your yardstick, and you take it for granted that because you've forced your yardstick upon others, that everyone is still using the same yardstick" (qtd. in Ambar 171). He argues that because the holders of power are changing, people who were not previously able to have a yardstick are now able to use their own yardstick to construct their reality. Therefore, one group's definition of a word will not have the same meaning for another group. Once cultures recognize this, they will better understand why groups use particular methods to shape their reality.

While Malcolm X used the yardstick metaphor to describe how cultures defined extremism, I believe the yardstick metaphor would also make a useful heuristic for WPAs when selecting educational materials for their courses. When administrators select or require textbooks for their courses, do they consider if or how these materials incorporate several yardsticks when anthologizing authors from marginalized cultures? Or do they use what I term *the yardstick of whiteness*—which I define as the reshaping of non-white authors into a one-dimensional framework—to make the marginalized writer/subject more palatable for white audiences? Using Malcolm X's "Hair" essay in the popular textbook, *Patterns for College Writing,* as an example, I argue that WPAs should review textbooks with more attention to how the yardstick of whiteness universalizes the experiences of African American subjects. Such attention has significance for the adoption, selection, and instruction of textbook materials, all of which shape writing programs and student experiences within these programs.

Measuring the Yardstick: Reading Malcolm X in *Patterns for College Writing*

The main noticeable instance of the yardstick of whiteness is in the biographical headnotes placed before the author's work. The headnotes serve as an introduction to the author's life and background for students. However, the background information typically repeats popular narratives about the author's life while eliminating how the yardstick of whiteness influenced the subject's life. This framing ultimately constructs the African American writer as an angry victim of racism or a person who succeeds despite racism. For instance, the editors in *Patterns* present Malcolm X as a lawless

Black man who finds religion, hates white Americans, has a religious epiphany, and is assassinated in a gang rivalry—essentially, the same yardstick used by the dominant culture when accessing Malcolm X's life. *Patterns* writes that Malcolm X experienced "a number of run-ins with the law" and "wound up in prison on burglary charges before he was twenty-one" (283). While in prison, he educated himself and joined Elijah Muhammad's "the Black Muslims" or now known as "the Nation of Islam," a "black separatist organization" (283). After leaving that organization, Malcolm X founded "a rival African-American political organization" (283). The biography presents a terse narrative and removes any information of how whiteness shaped Malcolm X's identity. For instance, his father is allegedly killed by white supremacists; the white state welfare agency separates his family after his mother's breakdown; and his prison sentence is stricter because of his associations with two white women. Likewise, stating that Malcolm X pursued his education in prison omits his formal education before he entered prison, an education that included a white teacher telling him that studying law was an unrealistic goal because of his race. Reading this header, students encounter a false and misleading biography that places the onus of race on the African American writer.

This burden of race continues with the false characterization of Muhammad's organization as Black Muslims, a moniker disliked by the sect. Officially, they were the Lost-Found Nation of Islam, and the contemporary Nation of Islam named in the headnote is not the same group Malcolm X joined.[1] The editors fail to name Malcolm X's organization—The Organization for Afro-American Unity—but settle on describing it as a rival to Muhammad's group, even though Malcolm X never viewed it this way. Labeling it as a rival group brings connotations connected to a gang, as if Malcolm X and Muhammad's groups were merely engaged in turf wars. Such connotations downplay, if not negate, the greater contributions each organization made to the African American Freedom Movement. Students, then, would be left with the impression of Malcolm X as the angry, dangerous Black man without recognizing how the white institutional practices shaped his ideology.

This haunting complexity of whiteness again occurs when *Patterns* presents cultural information before the reading, which is retitled as "My First Conk" instead of "Hair." Malcolm X argues in the narrative that one can gain agency through their body, and he provides commentary on how people condition themselves to view their body through the yardstick of another culture. Though the background on African American hairstyles offers readers the opportunity to learn about African American hair, the yardstick of whiteness primers readers to think that the main theme in both the headnote and "My First Conk" is the desire for African Americans to imitate whites. *Patterns* notes that the conk was a popular style for Black entertainers until the 1960s, when "more natural styles, including the Afro became a symbol of Black pride, and conked hair came to be seen as a self-loathing attempt to imitate whites" (283). *Patterns* does not mention that variations of the conk—texturizers, Jheri curls, S-curls, etc.—were popular hairstyles for African American men from the 1960s up to the present day. Even the wave cap—known as the do-rag—is another variation of the conk in an attempt to style one's hair. Students would miss the opportunity to learn that there is diversity within African American culture, and the textbooks reinforce a master narrative about African American life.

This one-dimensional presentation of African American life continues with the editors' description of "good" and "bad" hair. According to *Patterns*, "some contemporary African Americans still distinguish between 'good' (that is, naturally straight) and 'bad' (that is, naturally curly) hair" (283). This information is misleading because "good" hair can have various meanings other than "naturally straight." Wavy hair, for instance, is considered good hair, along with naturally curly hair. "Bad hair" generally means hair that is naturally tightly curled and hard to comb. Hairstyles in the Black community represent different things, depending on one's socioeconomic class. Manning Marable notes that in the 1940s—the era Malcolm X writes about in "Hair"—many middle-class African American men preferred wearing their hair in a short, natural style. The conk was a style representative of lower-class African Americans, "the emblem of the hippest, street-savvy Black, the choice of hustlers, pimps, professional gamblers, and criminals" (45). The yardstick of whiteness prevents any meaningful conversation about African American culture by creating narratives that are one-dimensional and avoid complexity. The African American student may not be able to relate to the narratives while the white student views the information as truthful without having any reference point to verify the information.

This simplification is reinforced in the following discussion question: "*The Autobiography of Malcolm X* was published in 1964, when many African Americans regularly straightened their hair. Is the thesis of this excerpt from the book still relevant today?" (286). According to the teacher's manual for *Patterns*, the main thesis of "Hair" is that "trying to look like a white man is degrading and that Blacks should concentrate on their brains, not their appearances, to get ahead" and that the theme of Black pride is still relevant today (61). Both the question and the answer place the burden of racism on the African American subject instead of the institution that created and fostered racist practices. It makes African Americans students feel that they have to defend their hairstyles without having white students understand how institutional racism created the need for Black pride which risks having African American students become the representative of a race that is highly diverse within its culture.

Advocating an Alternative: The Yardstick of Experience

As we all know, teaching materials, of which composition textbooks hold a significance place, affect both the manner in which students learn about writing and the pedagogy teachers use. These materials determine how students understand experiences and whether their in-class experiences are rewarding or detrimental to their future societal contributions. Rather than using educational materials based on the yardstick of whiteness, WPAs might develop a yardstick of experience to help them assess (or perhaps create) materials that present rich and complex contextual headnote and information. In the yardstick of experience, administrators will find materials that value the experiences of all students. To make sure that they use materials that contribute to the students' building and interpreting multi-dimensional experiences, WPAs should do the following:

Develop teacher-training sessions highlighting how to teach materials related to race and racism. If WPAs require programs to have a textbook for their course, they should offer substantial preparation to provide teachers with the necessary tools to discuss race and racism in the classroom. One technique would have teachers require students to review the world behind the text. Some questions asked would include: What was the specific racial history at the time the text was produced? What cultural events shaped the specific racial history? Where and how was the original text published? Who was the original audience for the text? If the original audience for the text was geared toward a specific race, what were some cultural literacies shared between the writer and the audience that students should know when reading the text? These questions would help teachers better prepare for class discussion and help students gain a more complex understanding of race and racism than the one provided by the textbook. As a result, the textbook would supplement the course material rather than become the dominant voice in the classroom.

Strongly encourage or request that publishers and editors of textbooks more accurately and fully represent the authors depicted. Publishers are an influential component in composition. They sponsor conferences, advertise in academic journals, survey teachers about educational products, and hire field representatives to market potential textbook adoptions for writing programs or individual instructors. Consequently, publishers promote textbooks that will have a lasting impact on the people who have to teach from it and the students who will have to read it. WPAs, then, should call for publishers to 1) diversify the editors who produce textbooks and 2) consult a diverse range of voices to create a more complex, detailed representation of groups in textbooks. Such representation would include headnotes showing how whiteness affects an author's life and providing multi-dimensional historical and cultural information. It would also include discussion questions that ask students to explore the complexities of race and white supremacy, helping students to see and build the yardstick of experience.

By acting on these and other initiatives, WPAs will help their programs begin the conversations about valuing the experiences of every cultural group instead of holding a yardstick of whiteness that privileges one group's belief on how students should read a racial group. Considering the complexity of headnotes in textbook adoption is just one of many areas in which WPAs should be attentive: The ways we represent and interpret the world influence all aspects of our writing programs and administrative work from professional development to the recruitment and retention of instructors and WPAs.

Notes

1. After Elijah Muhammad's death in 1975, his son Wallace Dean Muhammad leaned more toward orthodox Sunni Islam and allowed whites to become members. Lost-Found Nation of Islam was disbanded in the late 1970s and was later absorbed into mainstream Islam. Some members, under national spokesman Louis Farrakhan, formed a splinter organization that revived the original tenets of the Lost-Found Nation of Islam.

Works Cited

Ambar, Saladin. *Malcolm X at the Oxford Union: Racial Politics in a Global Era*. New York: Oxford UP, 2014. Print.

Kirszner, Laurie G., and Stephen R. Mandell, eds. *The Teacher's Manual for Patterns for College Writing, Brief Edition: A Rhetorical Reader and Guide*. 13th ed. Boston/New York: Bedford/St. Martin's, 2015. Print.

Malcolm X. *The Autobiography of Malcolm X: As Told to Alex Haley*. New York: Grove P, 1965. Print.

Marable, Manning. *Malcolm X: A Life of Reinvention*. New York: Penguin, 2011. Print.

Cedric Burrows is Assistant Professor of English at Marquette University, an urban, research-intensive Jesuit university. His research interests include African American rhetoric and social movement rhetoric. His current research project centers on how whiteness reframes the African American rhetorical presence in composition textbooks.

The Role of Composition Programs in De-Normalizing Whiteness in the University: Programmatic Approaches to Anti-Racist Pedagogies

James Chase Sanchez and Tyler S. Branson

It is well-known by now that the enrollment of college students in the US is changing. According to National Center for Educational Statistics, the next decade will see a 26% increase in Black student enrollment and a 26% increase in Hispanic student enrollment, as opposed to only a 4% increase in white students. However, college graduation rates remain steadily white. A recent report by the American Council of Education (ACE) found that "individuals who earned their baccalaureate degrees in 2007–2008 were not nearly as racially diverse as the overall undergraduate student body." Moreover, Ben Casselman, chief economics writer for the statistics website *FiveThirtyEight,* writes that "in 2013, about 40 percent of Whites between the ages of 25 and 29 had a bachelor's degree or more, compared to about 20 percent of Blacks, 15 percent of Hispanics and 58 percent of Asians." Casselman continues by adding these numbers suggest that "Blacks are catching up to Whites when it comes to going to college. But when it comes to finishing college and getting a degree, they are making much less progress." Casselman's piece illustrates a major theme that dominates many campuses across the US: Although many more people of color are entering college at two- and four-year institutions—and thus closing the gaps between students of color and white students—graduation rates for these groups seem to be stagnant.

These numbers challenge a commonly held assumption about college graduation rates, which is that income and parental education levels matter more in determining success in college than race or ethnicity. Daniel Fisher of *Forbes* claimed in 2012 that "millions of otherwise qualified high school students aren't attending college, either because they can't afford it or because the admissions system screens them out." Fisher follows others such as Korn and DeSilver who argue that income levels are the best indicators for admission to and graduation from college. However, other studies, such as one conducted from ACE, suggest race is actually a more important factor when graduation rates are considered. Mikyung Ryu, associate/interim director of ACE's policy analysis, states that we must take up new policies to help our minority students: "Given shifting student demographics," he writes, "this gap will likely widen unless we undertake serious efforts to eradicate barriers for nontraditional and disadvantaged minority students" (American Council on Education). Ryu's description of barriers might also be described as the normalization of whiteness, which presents obstacles that mostly students of color face. As writing instructors and writing program administrators, we want to urge the field to heed Ryu's call for action and combat the normalization of whiteness by investigating ways compositionists and WPAs can utilize their disciplinary expertise to better serve the changing student demographics in our own first-year composition classrooms.

We believe that first-year composition (FYC) can be a unique curricular space to resist the normalization of whiteness and better serve the changing demographic of college students. We can safely assume that the required writing course is one of the largest institutionalized curricula in the US, and as such, is in a unique position to impact a wide range of students at an institutional level. However, merely possessing an institutional space is not enough. For instance, a survey of California community colleges first reported at the 2009 CCCC meeting suggests that our nation's two-year colleges are unable to keep up with the rising demand of freshman English. At two-year colleges across California, the survey showed, FYC courses are suffering from overflowing class sizes, inflated teaching loads, and ever-increasing caps for remedial and non-remedial writing courses (Jaschik). *Inside Higher Ed* reported that the major impetus of the study, according to its authors, was "to document the educational consequences associated with failing to match educational needs with public support" (Jaschik). We are especially intrigued with this connection between educational needs and public support. In the case of the growing disparity between enrollment and graduation rates of minority students at our nation's two- and four-year colleges and universities, we need to make better arguments about the educational needs of our changing student body. Failing to do so will further maintain whiteness as the status quo, allowing more students of color to fall between the cracks. In addition, composition studies as a discipline would be apt to respond to those needs in ways that garner the kind of public support needed to make an impact. CCCC's "Principles for the Postsecondary Teaching of Writing," which suggests an ideal class size of 15 students, and no more than 60 students per semester, is a good start, but it doesn't go far enough in addressing how the changing demographic of FYC may necessitate a changing curriculum. For that matter, even with the "Principles for Postsecondary Teaching of Writing," for all its good intentions, we still are not in a good position to say for certain who is taking our courses, who is passing them, and whether or not they align with the troubling national numbers referenced above.

One common answer to the broader question of how composition as an academic discipline can be more responsive to public issues is perhaps the oldest one: relinquish freshman composition from its general education requirement. Sharon Crowley is most famous for this view, writing that freshman English, "since its beginnings in the late nineteenth century . . . has maintained an ethic of service" (227). K.J. Peters, moreover, argues that first-year composition, "more than any other college or university courses, serves as the *de facto* homeroom of higher education." Others, like Ira Shor, who called FYC the "linguistic gatekeeper" to upward mobility (92) or Sid Dobrin, echo the view that the field's relationship with the general education requirement hinders its ability both to effectively serve our students and to grow as a discipline. But we believe that no matter where you fall on this divisive debate, there are daily realities we all must confront, realities that are morphing and expanding before our eyes, realities that must be met with pragmatic and tangible solutions. In other words, despite the field's often problematic institutional relationship with FYC, we are nevertheless in a unique position to impact a wider student population and resist whiteness as the educational norm than perhaps any other discipline, and we think that should be an asset, not a hindrance.

The first approach we suggest for aligning FYC to address the changing racial dynamic of college students is to better understand how we deal with race in our own programs. Brij Mohan calls universities "vestiges of *white privilege* [that] continue to promote mediocrity on one hand and demoralization on the other" (2; emphasis original). By conducting more thorough analyses of individual composition programs across the country, we can better combat this pervasive institutionalization of white privilege while also giving us a better sense of the students who are taking our courses—who's passing, who's failing, and who's graduating—which will put us in a better position to address how our programs impact diverse student populations. In this issue, Cedric Burrows argues that one approach for harnessing FYC to combat whiteness as the educational norm is to reexamine how biographical headnotes in composition readers perpetuate whiteness as the norm. Other important work in this area comes from Poe et al., who analyzed how assessment practices impact changing student populations (589). They suggest an assessment strategy called disparate impact analysis as a self-study tool for multidisciplinary teams to implement less discriminatory assessment practices. We need more studies like these to discern both the educational needs of our students and also to garner the public support to address them effectively.

Second, we believe individual programs need to cultivate, nurture, and support curricular innovations or other pedagogical interventions that make room for nontraditional and/or disadvantaged minority students in the writing classroom. As Gary Weilbacher writes, failing to challenge curricular and institutional standards promotes and maintains whiteness as the status quo (5). One way we can make changes is to focus on how these issues intersect with graduate education and research in the field. Jasmine Tang and Noro Andriamanalina, for example, argue in this issue that universities need to develop broader institutional support for graduate students of color, and Sherri Craig critiques the field for not prioritizing narratives of WPAs of color. Following these scholars, we also need to consider undergraduate pedagogy, whether through interdisciplinary partnerships to better mentor writing students of color, as McManigell Grijalva details, or even through more focused workshops, demonstrations, and other forms of teacher training. This dedicated pedagogical commitment to destabilizing whiteness will not only help teachers elevate their consciousness in the classroom but also will aid in the kind of critical reflection necessary for more inclusive assignments and assessment practices from graduate to undergraduate levels. Elsewhere in the field, Terrance Tucker utilizes writing assignments that specifically deal with race, like his O.J. Simpson trial assignment, which asks students to analyze the opposite of their personal opinions on the O.J. verdict in the context of race and media perceptions, so "students can gain an appreciation of the significance of writing in critically shaping 'reality' and of the role that race, in particular, plays in constructing that social reality" (140). Reflexive assignments like Tucker's allow students and our programs to critique the structure of race and whiteness in society, applying a method of racialized consciousness that might not be applicable in other forms.

These, of course, are only a couple of tangible examples that could be employed in the classroom. As we said above, one of the primary motivations for programmatically addressing changing student demographics is to develop new ways to help match educational needs with public support. There are, ideally, multiple yet uncharted paths that can lead us to these discoveries. But there is even more at stake with this kind of work. For us, the goal is not just about identifying and addressing student needs in the composition classroom, it is also about reimagining the institutions we serve. In one of the foundational texts in critical race theory, "Whiteness as Property," Cheryl I. Harris claims that "American law has recognized a property interest in whiteness that, although unacknowledged, now forms the background against which legal disputes are framed, argued, and adjudicated" (277). Harris's explication of whiteness in legal doctrine leads us to reflect on how American education has established what George Lipsitz calls a "possessive investment in whiteness" too, one that dominates the universities and writing programs we inhabit. We argue that Harris's and Lipsitz's claims issue us a moral imperative to critically reorient our professional identities to combat institutional whiteness, not just in composition programs but within the university itself.

WORKS CITED

American Council on Education. "Report Finds Demographics of College Graduates Do Not Reflect Changes in Overall Student Body." *American Council on Education.* 16 May 2013. Web. 16 Oct. 2015.

Casselman, Ben. "Race Gap Narrows in College Enrollment." *FiveThirtyEight.com.* ESPN. 30 Apr. 2014. Web. 18 Oct. 2015.

Crowley, Sharon. "Composition's Ethic of Service, and the University Requirement, and the Discourse of Student Need." *Journal of Advanced Composition* 15.2 (1995): 227–39. Web. 12 Nov. 2015.

DeSilver, Drew. "College Enrollment Among Low-income Students Still Trails Richer Groups." *Pew Research Center.* The Pew Charitable Trusts. 15 Jan. 2014. Web. 21 Oct. 2015.

Dobrin, Sidney I. *Postcomposition.* Carbondale: Southern Illinois UP, 2011.

Fisher, Daniel. "Poor Students are the Real Victims of College Discrimination." *Forbes.com.* Forbes. 2 May 2012. Web. 27 Oct. 2015.

Harris, Cheryl I. "Whiteness as Property." *Critical Race Theory: The Key Writings that Formed the Movement.* Ed. Kimberle Crenshaw, Neil Gotanda, Gary Pellar, and Kendall Thomas. New York: The New Press, 1995. 276–91. Print.

Husser, William J., and Tabitha M. Bailey. "Projections for Education Statistics to 2021." 41st ed. *National Center for Education Statistics.* Institute of Educational Sciences, 2014. PDF.

Jaschik, Scott. "Composition, Overcrowded." *Inside Higher Ed.* 16 Mar. 2009. Web. 21 Oct. 2015.

Korn, Melissa. "Big Gap in College Graduation Rates for Rich and Poor." *Wall Street Journal.* Dow Jones & Company. 3 Feb. 2015. Web. 2 Nov. 2015.

Lipsitz, George: *The Possessive Investment in Whiteness: How White People Profit from Identity Politics.* Philadelphia: Temple UP, 2006. Print.

Mohan, Brij. "Rejoinder to 'Reinventing Social Work Education.'" *Research on Social Work Practice* 19.1 (2009): 116–18. Web. 15 Nov. 2015.

Peters, K.J. "A New Rhetorical Topography: How the Composition Classroom Became the University Homeroom and Where to Draw the Line." *Enculturation* 5.2 (2004). Web. 3 Nov. 2015.

Poe, Mya, Norbert Elliot, John Aloysius Cogan Jr., and Tito G. Nurudeen Jr. "The Legal and the Local: Using Disparate Impact Analysis to Understand the Consequences of Writing Assessment." *College Composition and Communication* 65.4 (2014): 588–611. Print.

"Principles for the Postsecondary Teaching of Writing." *NCTE: Conference on College Composition and Communication.* Rev. Mar. 2015. Web. 27 Oct. 2015.

Shor, Ira. "Our Apartheid: Writing Instruction and Inequality." *Journal of Basic Writing* 16.1 (1997): 91–104. Print.
Tucker, Terrance. "Teaching Race to Students Who Think the World is Free." *Pedagogy* 6.1 (2006): 133–40. Web. 1 Nov. 2015.
Weilbacher, Gary. "Standardization and Whiteness: One and the Same?" *Democracy and Education* 20.2 (2012): 1–7. *JSTOR*. Web. 6 Nov. 2015.

James Chase Sanchez is a fourth-year doctoral candidate in Rhetoric and Composition at Texas Christian University, a private Research 2 school, where he is currently completing his dissertation, "Preaching Behind the Fiery Pulpit: Rhetoric, Self-Immolation, and Public Memory." His research situates race within public memory, and he is especially interested in the ways the two construct (counter)narratives. His work has appeared in Present Tense *and* Steinbeck Review, *and he is also a 2015 winner of the Scholar for the Dream Award for CCCC.*

Tyler S. Branson is a Lecturer in the Writing Program at the University of California Santa Barbara, a public R1 university. His research focuses broadly on how people use rhetoric and writing to collaborate with one another to address public problems, particularly in the context of higher education. His most recent work is forthcoming in the edited collections Cambridge Handbook of Service Learning and Civic Engagement *by Cambridge University Press and* Writing and Composing in the Age of MOOCs *by IGI Global.*

On Keeping Score: Instructors' vs. Students' Rubric Ratings of 46,689 Essays

Joseph M. Moxley and David Eubanks

ABSTRACT

This study investigates the efficacy of having first-year composition students score one another's intermediate drafts of essays using a five-trait rubric across 482 sections of two introductory composition courses (ENC1101 and ENC1102).[1] This study analyzes 46,689 reviews, which consisted of 16,312 reviews conducted by instructors and 30,377 reviews conducted by students. The papers, typically between 1,000 and 1,500 words each, were written by students over the course of seven semesters at University of South Florida, a state university in the United States. We found low to modest correlations between peer ratings and instructor ratings on individual assignments. On average, peers assigned higher ratings than instructors, yet, over time, students' scores were more highly correlated with instructors' scores. The average differences in ratings between the students and instructors were smallest for Focus *and* Format *and greatest for* Evidence. *Students who received higher ratings on their own writing from instructors provided scores that had a broader range of scores and were more highly correlated with instructors' scores than students who received lower scores from instructors. Generally, peers had a smaller rating variance of scores than instructors.*

While a good many pedagogical essays have been published regarding best classroom practices for conducting peer review, surprisingly little quantitative, replicable, aggregated, data-driven (RAD) research has been conducted on peer review in the discipline of Writing Studies. Regarding the paucity of empirical research in NCTE journals, Richard Haswell concluded that "peer critique seems to be one of the least studied of practices now very common in college writing classrooms" (211). One overlooked question is whether or not it is worthwhile to have students assess other students using a rubric. While a few studies have compared instructor scores to student scores to interrogate the validity of peer review, to reach the effects of training on peer reviews, or to investigate gender bias in peer review, these studies have been limited by small sample sizes. To our knowledge, only one of these studies questioned if the correlation between instructor and student scores changes over time or whether reviewers are more likely to reach higher levels of correlation for particular rubric criteria.

At the first-year composition program (FYC) at the University of South Florida, we are especially interested in this question because we would like to know whether it is a worthwhile practice to require students to score one another's intermediate drafts. We also wanted to evaluate whether our practice of using one generic rubric across sections of two composition courses was working well. The FYC rubric had been developed via a crowdsourcing process conducted by writing instructors, writing program administrators, and USF's Office of Institutional Effectiveness (Vierrege et al.). Past research addressed the internal reliability of the numeric rubric (Moxley, "Aggregated Assessment"); illustrated ways writing program administrators have deployed the numeric rubric to make real-time, evidence-based curriculum enhancements (Langbehn et al.; Moxley, "Big Data"); and analyzed instructors' and students' use of rubric criteria in 118,611 comments made on 17,433 student essays (Dixon and Moxley).[2] While we identified benefits to having instructors and students use the same rubric across genres and courses (Moxley, "Big Data"; Anson et al., "Theorizing Community"), we were troubled by how our policies contradicted modern assessment theory—that is, the assumption that every rhetorical situation warrants a unique rubric (Anson et al., "Big Rubrics"). We wondered whether we could better serve our students by using different rubrics for different genres and purposes. Initially, My Reviewers, the tool we use to markup student documents and to conduct peer reviews and team projects, didn't permit customizable rubrics. But after that particular technical obstacle was overcome, we wondered if we should revisit the possibility of diverse, multiple, project-specific rubrics for peer reviews (see http://myreviewers.com for software details). When we broached this possibility with our instructors and colleagues, we faced some resistance, so we wanted to research the efficacy of our existing measures before considering the move to multiple rubrics or discontinuing the practice of asking students to score as well as comment on peers' works.[3]

In summary, this study uses corpus methods to investigate the efficacy of having students score one another's essays as opposed to solely providing textual comments. In particular, we analyze the rubric scores provided by instructors and students who used the numeric version of the FYC rubric to assess intermediate drafts—that is, 16,312 reviews provided by 107 instructors and 30,377 peer reviews provided by 5,857 students—for the three major projects in two introductory composition courses between the spring 2012 and spring 2014 semesters.[4] Through our exploration, we sought to mainly explore these questions:

1. Would students score similarly to their instructors?

2. Would the correlation between students' scores with instructors' scores improve over time (within a class and over the year in both composition courses) and why might that be the case?

3. Is peer scoring an effective pedagogical practice?

4. What changes to our curriculum—including our implementation of the rubric, the design of the rubric, the training of students to prepare them for peer review—are suggested by study results?

Literature Review

In the discipline of Writing Studies, empirical work on peer review has been sparse, especially given the popularity of this pedagogical practice. So little empirical work has been published in the flagstaff publications of the Conference on College Composition and Communication and the National Council of Teachers of English, in fact, that Richard Haswell contended in 2005 that Writing Studies was at war with "empirical inquiry, laboratory studies, data gathering, experimental investigation, formal research, hard research, and sometimes just research" (200). Outside of Writing Studies, however, in the broader assessment and education literature, research on peer review has been fairly robust. In his literature review spanning 1980 to 1996, Keith Topping used the search terms "*peer assessment, peer marking, peer correction, peer rating, peer feedback, peer review,* and *peer appraisal* (together with university, college, and higher education")" ("Peer Assessment" 250) to find 109 publications that focused on peer review in the Social Science Citation Index, Dissertation Abstracts International, and ERIC databases. Of those 109 studies, 67 articles "included outcome data gathered in an orderly research process" (250). Regarding the validity and reliability of peers' assessments, Topping concluded, "Peer assessment of writing and peer assessment using marks, grades, and tests have shown positive formative effects on student achievement and attitudes; these effects are as good as or better than the effects of teacher assessment" (249). Interestingly, in the 25 studies that compared teachers' marks or grades with students', researchers reported high reliability between teachers and students in 18 (72%) of the studies (257).

Using Topping's same search terms in ISI Web of Science (formerly the Social Science Citation Index), we found 23 empirical studies had been published on peer review between 1997 and July of 2014. Continuing the trend identified by Haswell, all of these RAD studies were published in non-NCTE journals.[5] These research studies address a range of topics (e.g., peer review and gender, experiences of L2 students, attitudes toward peer review, effects of training, and validity of peer reviews versus self-assessment or teacher assessment) and methods (survey, observational, quasi-experimental, and meta-analysis). One fairly robust theme in the literature is the question of gender bias in peer reviews, and these studies have occasionally compared peers' and instructors scores by gender (Tucker; Falchikov and Magin). Several studies have compared students' and instructors' scores on papers to interrogate the validity of peer reviews (Falchikov and Boud; Falchikov and Goldfinch). Liu and Lu found that after receiving training in peer review strategies, the correlation between students' scores and instructors' scores significantly increased. Esfandiari and Myford compared the ratings on an eight-point analytical scale provided by 194 assessors on 188 essays and found that teachers were most critical, then peer assessors, and then self assessors. When Liang and Tsai compared self, peer, and expert assessments on a four-point analytic scale (Knowledge, Suitability, Correctness, and Creativity) to assess biology reports written by 47 students, they found good consistency between students and experts and found that interrater agreement improved over time.

Perhaps due to the limitations of traditional data collection techniques, one important limitation of past research on peer review in general has been that it has been primarily constrained by small sample sizes.[6] Excluding Takeda and Homberg's study, which analyzed the peer reviews of 1,001 British students, and Tucker's 2014 study of gender in peer review with a sample of 1,523 students, no large-scale empirical work has been conducted on peer review. Instead, past empirical investigations have been limited—sample sizes are typically fewer than 50 (Khonbi and Sadeghi; Liu and Lee; Liu and Li; Lundstrom and Baker). Only five studies have worked with samples of more than 200 students (see table 1).

Table 1
Largest quantitative sampling plan for studies on peer review, 1997-2014

N (students)	Study	Method	Finding(s)
1,523	Tucker (2014)	Group mean comparison	Absence of gender bias in peer assessments Women received significantly higher peer ratings than men (p < .05)
1,001	Takeda & Homberg (2014)	Individual level comparison Group mean comparison	Gender balanced groups show notably lower variation in self- and peer-assessment scores Enhanced collaboration between students in gender balanced groups
300	Boase-Jelinek, Parker, & Herrington (2013)	Individual level comparison	Students did not interpret the rubric in a similar manner as their tutor.
211	Patchan, Schunn, & Clark (2011)	Group mean comparison Correlation	Students' drafts were of higher quality when written for peers than when written for their teacher's assistant Students provided more detailed reviewer comments than teaching assistants However, between student and TA reviewers, only moderate differences were found in final draft scores
208	Crossman & Kite (2012)	Individual level comparison	Use of rubrics with peer reviews resulted in improved quality of students' papers between the initial and final drafts.

Research Design

In this study, we use statistical measures to compare instructors' scores on intermediate drafts with students' scores on these same drafts. Instructors and students used the numeric version of the FYC rubric to score intermediate and final drafts.

Setting

Over a three-year period, 128 instructors used My Reviewers to assign students to peer review groups, typically two or three students per group. The papers students were asked to review constituted the primary coursework/grades for two composition courses (ENC1101 and ENC1102): annotated bibliographies, literature reviews, analytic essays, historiographies, Rogerian arguments, remediations, and arguments for social justice. We offer three versions of ENC1101: a completely online model, a traditional model wherein students meet in classes (with enrollments capped at 25/class during the fall and 22/class during the spring), and a flipped model, wherein students meet for about an hour in large groups each week and then meet two hours either one-on-one with instructors or in small groups. We offer two versions of ENC1102: traditional and online. While the nature of these courses changed somewhat from year to year, the three projects in each course were designed to be increasingly more difficult, moving from summary to synthesis to argument (see http://fyc.usf.edu/~hosted for project details). All students were required to write three drafts of each project: 1) a preliminary draft that the instructor and student discussed, typically in a one-on-one conference; 2) an intermediate draft that the instructor and students reviewed independently; and 3) a final draft that only the instructor reviewed. Regardless of which type of class they were enrolled in, all students conducted their peer reviews anonymously online, using My Reviewers. In total, during this time period, first-year composition instructors reviewed 16,312 intermediate drafts and students reviewed 30,377 intermediate drafts using the numeric version of the FYC rubric.

Given that we are a fairly large community comprised primarily of graduate students who have disparate teaching schedules and that our curriculum already takes 10 hours to teach each week—the number of hours for which we pay our graduate students each week—it would be unreasonable to ask for more time from our instructors. We have found it nearly impossible to host grade-and-comment norming sessions although we recognize the value of such sessions in terms of facilitating stronger inter-rater reliability among instructors in our program. Beyond approximately 24 hours of training in our yearly fall orientation, grade norming is limited to the new graduate students who enter our program each year and who are required to take a semester-long practicum that meets weekly. To help facilitate a shared language for assessment and response, therefore, we have provided a variety of peer-review videos and sample document markups in the three ebooks we have developed for our students.

All students used My Reviewers to conduct their peer reviews. Generally, our instructors graded and commented on intermediate drafts at the same time students conducted peer reviews on the same intermediate drafts. However, a few instructors required students to rewrite their projects after the peers' reviews and before they graded or responded to them. In addition, there were some additional variances regarding ways instructors used My Reviewers. For example, some instructors simply assigned the peer reviews and neglected to grade them; others graded the peer reviews but did not discuss them in class; some broke the anonymity of the peer reviews as experienced at My Reviewers and asked students to conduct follow up face-to-face sessions in class after their online peer reviews; some discussed peer review in class meetings, as recommended by our sample detailed schedule, but others did not.

When using My Reviewers, instructors and students have a range of features that they may or may not utilize. For example, students and instructors may use the .pdf-markup tools to write comments and draw on the papers; write endnotes that explained their in-text comments; and place Community Comments on one another's documents, which are hyperlinks out to an article, video, and *Try It! Exercises* about the comments.[7] Within the My Reviewers document-workflow system, instructors may view from a single page all aggregated sticky notes, endnotes, Community Comments, and rubric scores each student provided on assigned peer reviews (see figure 1). Below that information, instructors may grade peer reviews and write a note to the student regarding his or her review. Instructors may also double click to see each peer review from the student view.[8] Adoption of these features has been varied across instructors.

Instrumentation

The community rubric all instructors and students used during the conduct of this investigation contains five broad categories—*Focus, Evidence, Organization, Style,* and *Format*. Three of the rubric criteria—*Focus, Organization,* and *Style*—contain two subcategories: *Basics* and *Critical Thinking*. *Evidence* includes the *Critical Thinking* subcategory whereas *Format* includes *Basics*. The *Basics* subcategory focuses on language conventions such as grammar, mechanics, and punctuation, while the *Critical Thinking* subcategory identifies global rhetorical concerns.

Instructor Overall Comment
You made some good observations on your peers' papers. However, there are times when your comments are a little vague and might not be as useful to your peers. For instance, at one point you wrote: "Nice work here!" It would be more helpful to explain exactly what part of your peer's writing was done well. Finally, please be sure to add comments in all of the criteria text boxes. These can be very helpful in letting your peers know what larger, global changes they need to make to their papers.

Instructor Grade: B

Peer Review Written By	Reviewer Rubric Comments	Reviewer In-Text Comments
Reviewer 1 View This Peer Review	**Evidence:** Most of your sources are appropriate/credible for scholarly research. You just need to check the reliability of the one I noted in your paper. Overall though, well done! **Analysis:** You meet most of the assignment requirements, however you needed one more section on what potential counterarguments could be made against your claim. Also, your research question is too broad/narrow, needs development, and lacks focus. You are on the	(1) Nice work here! (2) Your thesis statement could be clearer. I feel like you do a good job defending your points in the body of your paper, but that your thesis does not encompass all of your points. I think that you should reread your paper so that you can formulate a thesis that matches your final argument. (3) Excellent point! This is interesting how you incorporated our
Reviewer 2 View This Peer Review	**Analysis:** Your analysis is on the right track, but lacking somewhat. You haven't met all of the assignment requirements, particularly you need to have another paragraph discussing the importance of some of the topics discussed in class. Moreover, your intro is a bit weak and doesn't fully incorporate everything you discuss in the body of the paper. **Format/Organization:** Your paper is correctly formatted.	(1) I feel like you can expand on this intro and split it into two paragraphs. (2) Your thesis is on the right track, but needs work. Your thesis is very broad and general, but your actual argument is quite specific. (3) I like your use of sources. However you seem to discuss them mostly in one paragraph. I might break that up a bit. (4) This is a really interesting point. Maybe you could expand on it
Reviewer 3 View This Peer Review	**Evidence:** You've found some really great sources! However, it seems like you rely heavily on one source for the majority of the paper. I would find some different sources to use throughout. Otherwise, well done. **Style:** You've done a good job with this criteria. You have a few punctuation errors, but otherwise, there are no real issues. You might vary your sentence length a bit more, but this is more about personal preference.	(1) I think that you may want to switch this paragraph and the one before it. This paragraph seems to relate more to your point earlier in the paper. (2) You may want to rework your thesis (3) I feel like you need to better transition into this next paragraph.

Fig. 1. Sample peer review and instructor grade of a review.

During the early part of the study—spring 2012 through fall 2013—instructors could choose between two versions of the community rubric when assigning peer review: the numeric rubric, which requires students to score rubric criteria on a five-point scale, and the discuss rubric, which requires students to write textual comments regarding these criteria rather than scores. When presented a choice, instructors have favored the numeric version of the FYC rubric over the discuss version, perhaps because the numeric version is the default rubric defined by the My Reviewers system or perhaps because students who are required to take the composition classes are often grade focused and prefer to know where they stand grade-wise at the intermediate draft stage. During the spring 2014, instructors were only presented with the numeric rubric option (see table 2).

Research Limitations

Beyond the rubric scores, students and instructors provided on intermediate drafts reported on in this study, reviewers provided written comments, including .pdf sticky notes and drawings and text notes on top of students' papers, rubric-based comments, Community Comments, summary notes, and revision plans. However, given scope limitations, this study does not provide an analysis of these lexical comments nor does it compare improvement from intermediate to final projects. In addition, given the limitation of the IRB protocol that we followed for this study, we do not analyze students' scoring by students' gender, SAT scores, college or high school grades, ethnicity, or First Time in College status.[9] Finally, it is important to note that this is a purely observational study, and, following Schneider et al., we make no claims about causality.

Results

This study reveals large differences between instructors' and students' scores on intermediate drafts written as the primary coursework for two introductory composition courses. Generally speaking, students score higher than instructors, particularly in the first project in ENC1101, although over time the correlation between students' and instructors' scores improves.

What Is the Agreement between Instructor- and Peer-Assigned Ratings?

Assuming instructors' reviews represent the gold standard, it follows that close association between peer and instructor scores indicates desirable metacognitive skills on the part of students with regard to assessing writing and presumably leads to better writers.

Table 2
The Common Rubric for First-Year Composition

Criteria	Level	Emerging 0	Developing 2		Mastering 4
			1	3	
Focus	Basics	Does not meet assignment Requirements	Partially meets assignment requirements		Meets assignment requirements
	Critical Thinking	Absent or weak thesis; ideas are underdeveloped, vague or unrelated to thesis; poor analysis of ideas relevant to thesis	Predictable or unoriginal thesis; ideas are partially developed and related to thesis; inconsistent analysis of subject relevant to thesis		Insightful/intriguing thesis; ideas are convincing and compelling; cogent analysis of subject relevant to thesis
Evidence	Critical Thinking	Sources and supporting details lack credibility; poor synthesis of primary and secondary sources/evidence relevant to thesis; poor synthesis of visuals/personal experience/anecdotes relevant to thesis; rarely distinguishes between writer's ideas and source's ideas	Fair selection of credible sources and supporting details; unclear relationship between thesis and primary and secondary sources/evidence; ineffective synthesis of sources/evidence relevant to thesis; occasionally effective synthesis of visuals/personal experience/anecdotes relevant to thesis; inconsistently distinguishes between writer's ideas and source's ideas		Credible and useful sources and supporting details; cogent synthesis of primary and secondary sources/evidence relevant to thesis; clever synthesis of visuals/personal experience/anecdotes relevant to thesis; distinguishes between writer's ideas and source's ideas.
Organization	Basics	Confusing opening; absent, inconsistent, or non-relevant topic sentences; few transitions and absent or unsatisfying conclusion	Uninteresting or somewhat trite introduction, inconsistent use of topics sentences, segues, transitions, and mediocre conclusion		Engaging introduction, relevant topic sentences, good segues, appropriate transitions, and compelling conclusion

Table 2 cont.
The Common Rubric for First-Year Composition

Criteria	Level	Emerging 0	Developing 2	Mastering 4
	Critical Thinking	Illogical progression of supporting points; lacks cohesiveness	Supporting points follow a somewhat logical progression; occasional wandering of ideas; some interruption of cohesiveness	Logical progression of supporting points; very cohesive
Style	Basics	Frequent grammar/punctuation errors; inconsistent point of view	Some grammar/punctuation errors occur in some places; somewhat consistent point of view	Correct grammar and punctuation; consistent point of view
	Critical Thinking	Significant problems with syntax, diction, word choice, and vocabulary	Occasional problems with syntax, diction, word choice, and vocabulary	Rhetorically-sound syntax, diction, word choice, and vocabulary; effective use of figurative language
Format	Basics	Little compliance with accepted documentation style (i.e., MLA, APA) for paper formatting, in-text citations, annotated bibliographies, and works cited; minimal attention to document design	Inconsistent compliance with accepted documentation style (i.e., MLA, APA) for paper formatting, in-text citations, annotated bibliographies, and works cited; some attention to document design	Consistent compliance with accepted documentation style (i.e., MLA, APA) for paper formatting, in-text citations, annotated bibliographies, and works cited; strong attention to document design

We began our analysis by examining the inter-rater properties between peers and instructors. Inter-rater reliability is an assessment of how well two or more raters implicitly rank each observation relative to the others (do they rise and fall together?). On average, individual raters may tend to assign higher or lower scores than others and still agree on ranking, which we measure with correlation of average scores across each peer-reviewed paper (see fig. 2).

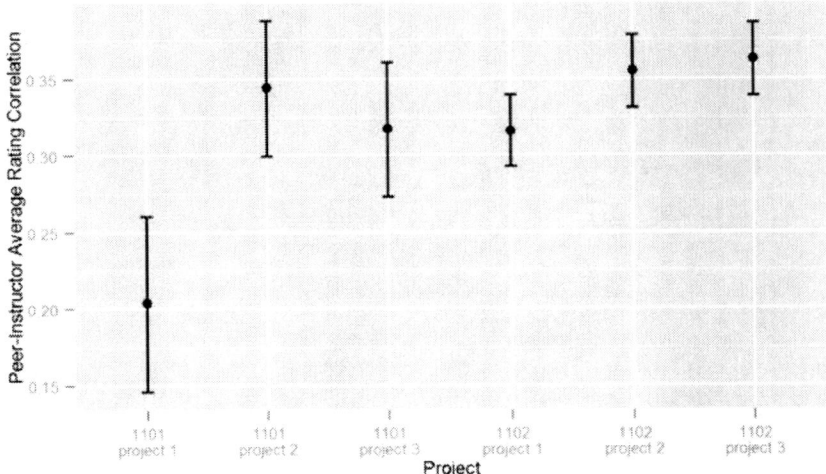

Fig. 2. Peer review instructor average rating by project.

The correlations in figure 2 are between the average score over the eight sub-scores for peer ratings and instructor ratings on samples sizes of greater than 1000 for ENC1101 and greater than 5000 for ENC1102. The dot in the middle is the estimated correlation, and the upper and lower range shown with the bars are 95% confidence intervals. The correlations are low to modest, but in addition to showing that there is some relationship between student rater and instructor on individual papers, the sequence shows that raters improve this correspondence after the first project in ENC1101. When we compare the intervals graphed in figure 2, we can see that the differences between correlations show a large gap between the first project of ENC1101 and the subsequent projects ($p < .002$, $z > 3.1$ for each of these comparisons). The numerical differences between the subsequent projects are not statistically significant. This suggests that there probably is some unique aspect of the first assignment in ENC1101 that produces lower student-instructor rating agreement. For example, perhaps the first assignment in ENC1101 teaches students how to better conform to rating norms.

We next visually compared the average ratings of peers and instructors by graphing the two together. The average score can range from zero to four, and if the scores matched perfectly, the graph would just be points marked by circles (one per student) that fall on the diagonal line from zero to four. We already know from the correlation analysis that the agreement isn't perfect, so realistically we expect a cloud of points, and the shape of the cloud may have some interest to us (see fig. 3).

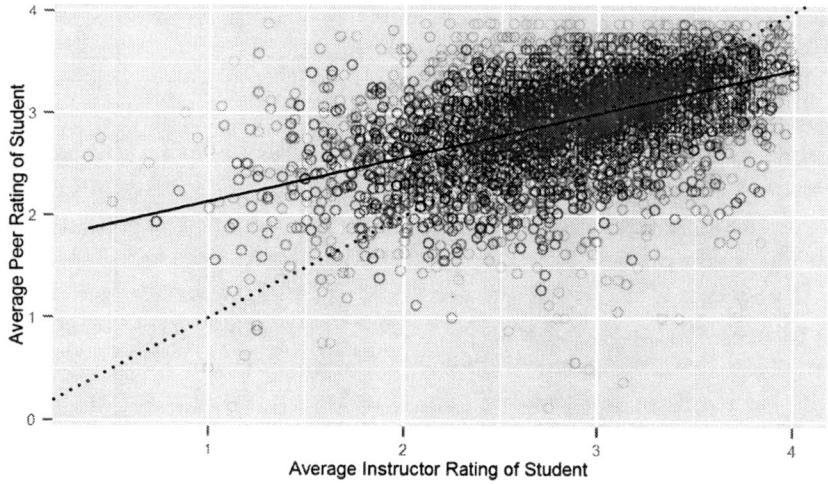

Fig. 3. Scatterplot comparing instructor ratings to peer ratings.

The scatterplot in figure 3 has a circular mark to denote each student's average scores assigned by the instructor (horizontal scale) and peers (vertical scale). We can see that most of these points fall between an average of 2 and about 3.8 in both cases, which means that zeros and ones are being reserved for exceptionally poor (or incomplete) papers. This is good news for the students, whose grades depend on these scores, but it is less optimal from a measurement point of view because it squashes the measurements together and makes it harder to distinguish cases. This undoubtedly contributes to the low correlation between peer and instructor scores.

The dotted diagonal line shows where peers and instructors agree on the score for a given student. There is substantial disagreement, but a linear regression model can find the straight line through the cloud of points that fits the data as well as any straight line can do. The result is the solid line on the graph, and the technical details are as follows: $R^2 = .21$, $F(1, 5776) = 1580$ ($p<.001$). Comparing that to the dotted perfect match reference line, we can see that peers have a tendency to rate higher than instructors for average ratings less than 3 and rate somewhat lower than instructors for ratings greater than 3.

An analysis of inter-rater agreement shows that peer raters have a hard time distinguishing between the 3 versus 4 rating on the scale. That is, the distinction appears to be statistically random. This is less true for the 1 versus 2 ratings, implying that students do have some skill in making quality distinctions, but that this ability is commensurate with their own development as a writer. The good news is that peers had a relatively easy time distinguishing the 1s from 4s, so their powers of discrimination do exist, but perhaps not at the finest level of the rubric.

Taken together, these findings suggest several ways to generate higher quality peer ratings. One is to combine training with pedagogy (e.g. using a rubric as a teaching tool) and more narrowly focus on specific aspects of writing within a given assignment. For example, instead of using the generic rubric, a simpler one with narrower characteristics may allow inexpert raters to more easily identify the traits on the rubric. Pedagogical use could also extend to training assignments where students rate pre-scored samples to see if they get the correct score. Finally, the issue of which end of the rubric to concentrate on seems to emerge from these findings. That is, do we build on the seeming natural ability of students to distinguish poor from average work (or whatever we call the low end of the scale), or do we work harder to simultaneously develop their writing with the metacognitive skills required to distinguish good from excellent work? This is, in itself, an interesting research question. We believe it is reasonable to assume that being a good critic is actually harder than being a good writer, and we might want to plan the curricular path of peer review to incorporate this lag. It also raises the question of whether peer reviews could do more harm than good in responding to good or excellent work. Perhaps, after all, students should not be asked to score papers but instead provide lexical comments, although without more research we cannot be sure about the veracity of their lexical comments.

Finally, regarding classroom implications, it is important to note that these results suggest the quality of reviews is more likely to be linked to the strength of the writers in each group rather than the total number of students in a group, given stronger writers had a broader spread of scores and a higher correlation of scores in relation to their instructors' scores on their papers. Hence, writing instructors should give some thought to the quality of writers in a group and not just the size of the group.

How Do Instructors' Scores by Rubric Criteria Compare with Students' Scores by Rubric Criteria on Intermediate Drafts?

In figure 3, we saw that peers tend to rate higher than instructors when the average is less than 3 and lower than instructors otherwise. We now investigate the differences for each of the eight rubric traits. Close association between the peer and instructor ratings indicates desirable metacognitive skills on the part of students with regard to assessing writing and that presumably leads to better writers. Therefore, the differences between peer and instructor ratings may tell us relative strengths and weaknesses of particular traits within the rubric (see fig. 4).

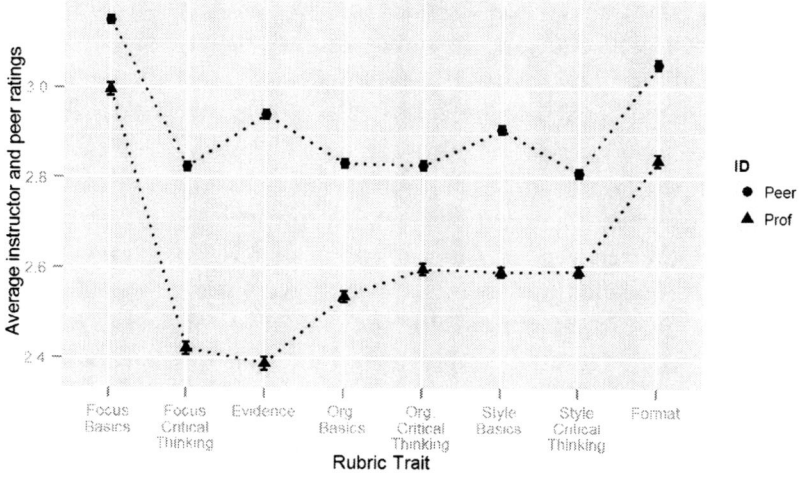

Fig. 4. Average instructor and peer ratings by rubric trait.

Figure 4 shows that, on average, peer reviewers rate higher than instructors on every trait. We can see from the confidence intervals that the differences are all statistically significant (because the error bars are not overlapping), and using Welch's t-test of difference of means, each difference has $p <$ .001. The difference between peer and instructor is least for *Focus 1* (which assesses the degree to which the text addresses the assignment prompt) and *Format*, which are arguably the easiest traits to assess. In contrast, *Focus: Critical Thinking* and *Evidence* have the largest gaps. The former is not surprising since it is probably the most complex of all the traits that students are asked to assess. *Evidence* seems much easier to identify. Here again, a developmental model of writing and metacognition would be useful. We make the tentative, but we think reasonable, conclusion that student and instructor ratings are best aligned when the trait being assessed is simple and therefore easier for a novice to identify.

Do Better Writers Score More Similarly to Instructors than Weaker Writers?

We calculated the overall score received by each student from his or her instructor as a proxy for expressed writing ability and divided the students into quartiles from lowest to highest. Within each of these ranks, we computed the correlation of scores those students gave as peers to the scores assigned by instructors on the same papers, using the average of the eight rubric subscores for comparison. The lowest ability peer raters (as measured by the scores on their own papers) have a .25 to .31 correlation with their instructors when rating the same papers. In contrast, the highest ability peer raters have a confidence interval of .34 to .40 (all correlations are different from zero with $p<.001$). This difference between the lowest and highest quartile is significant ($p < .001$). This trend suggests that—as one would expect—students who receive better ratings on their own writing from their teachers make better peer reviewers, assuming, again, that the instructors' score represents the gold standard. The correlations are low in absolute terms, and we have already seen that the peer ratings have several validity issues, but the large number of samples allows us to detect this slight tendency of increased alignment between instructors and the best writers. There is one other element of this agreement that is worth mentioning: Statistically, correlations tend to increase as the variance, or *spread*, of ratings increases. We already noticed that the limited use of the full range of the 0-4 scale presents research problems, and the same is true of individual raters. To illustrate, imagine a rater who only ever assigns a 3. In effect, no information is transmitted with these ratings because they cannot distinguish between levels of quality. Overall, peers had a smaller rating variance (median = .24) than instructors (median = .42), meaning that peer ratings provide less information for either feedback or assessment purposes than do instructors, and the disparity serves to lower the correlations between peers and instructors. Assigning a wider spread of ratings is presumably a trainable skill and could even be enforced in an online system (imagine having only a limited number of 4s to hand out, for example). At the least, the awareness of score spread can be reinforced by reporting it to raters as they rate. We envision this conscious discrimination and feedback as a general teamwork skill with applications in many types of collaboration.

Do We Really Need Eight Rubric Traits?

Peer reviewers could understandably have trouble distinguishing between the eight distinct ratings they assign, each of which is supposed to assess a different aspect of a paper. In fact, we cannot expect even the best raters to cleanly distinguish between them. We can imagine a paper that has perfect organization but is utterly lacking in style or a paper that is formatted to perfection but lacks an evidentiary basis. However, when we mix together eight of these traits (or dimensions), it is to be expected that relationships between them become evident. One way to detect that is to simply look at the correlations between scores assigned to the eight individual traits (see table 3).

Table 3
Correlation Matrix of Rubric Traits for Peer Ratings (n = 30,377)

	1	2	3	4	5	6	7	8
1. Focus (Basics)	-							
2. Focus (Critical Thinking)	.61	-						
3. Evidence (Critical Thinking)	.56	.55	-					
4. Organization (Basics)	.54	.60	.63	-				
5. Organization (Critical Thinking)	.48	.50	.44	.48	-			
6. Style (Basics)	.48	.47	.53	.51	.40	-		
7. Style (Critical Thinking)	.47	.54	.51	.58	.44	.67	-	
8. Format (Basics)	.45	.38	.45	.42	.41	.43	.42	-

p<.001 for all correlations

If the traits behaved independently from one another, so that each of them could vary without affecting the others, we would see a very different pattern from the correlations in table 3. Namely, all the entries would be zero (the dashes indicate 1s, to indicate that a trait is trivially correlated with itself).

There are two possibilities to explain the fact that the correlations are not close to zero. One is that writers tend to produce papers such that if they are good in one area, they are good in another area, e.g. organization and style. The other explanation is that the peer reviewers have trouble distinguishing between the categories they are to rate and conflate them. There is no way to know with the data on hand which of these is the case, but it is probably a combination of the two explanations.

The next level of analysis is to delve within the correlation table and look for groups of traits that clump together within the ratings. For example, looking at table 3 again, we notice that all of the correlations are positive—

they all tend to go up together or down together. As an analogy, if we were to measure the height, length, weight, and food consumption of our pets, we would probably find that all these dimensions go up or down together, corresponding to the overall size of the pet. It turns out that the eight rubric ratings are predominately driven by a kind of size, which we take to be a holistic quality of the paper (see table 4).

The columns of table 4 give information for both peer ratings and instructor ratings. The most important figures are the component 1 columns. The top row shows that over half the variance in the eight individual trait scores is captured with a single number. Notice that the decimal numbers in each of the component 1 columns are nearly identical—all of them are around .3 to .4. This means that the main size component of the ratings is almost exactly a simple average of the eight individual scores. Interestingly, this is also how the grade is calculated for the paper.

There is little difference in this tendency between peers and instructors. It stretches the imagination to think that in the writing assignments, each of these eight traits would naturally progress at the same rate. We would expect some differences in development; maybe organization develops faster than style, for example. This tilts the explanation toward the other possibility, that raters are influenced by a holistic or average sense of the quality of the work and assign the eight individual ratings informed by that impression. If this is the case, then the rubric probably doesn't really need eight traits. Evaluating eight rubric criteria 46,689 times—that is, making 373,512 evaluations—represents a great deal of effort.

Ultimately, then, this finding challenges the notion that holistic scoring is invariably less helpful and precise than analytical rubrics. Clearly, there are strengths and weaknesses to analytic-trait scoring and holistic scoring: With the analytic approach, instructors may intuit the overall grade and work backwards to fill in rubric scores. This gives them a numerical explanation for grades assigned and, in theory, tells the student what he or she needs to improve. By contrast, the holistic/contrast approach would sacrifice this bookkeeping justification to some extent but also free up the instructor to give a wider range of feedback. It also makes measuring and training inter-rater reliability easier because there is only one holistic score to agree on, and more freedom can be granted to the contrasting strengths and weaknesses, as well as creative rule-breaking.

Table 4
Principle Components Analysis of Rubric Traits, First Two Dimensions

	Peer Ratings (n=30,377)		Instructor Ratings (n= 16,312)	
	Component 1	Component 2	Component 1	Component 2
Proportion of Variance	56%	9%	58%	11%
Focus (Basics)	.36	.30	.34	.40
Focus (Critical Thinking)	.37	.21	.38	.22
Evidence (Critical Thinking)	.37	-	.36	.26
Organization (Basics)	.38	-	.39	-
Organization (Critical Thinking)	.32	.48	.39	-
Style (Basics)	.35	-.58	.33	-.61
Style (Critical Thinking)	.37	-.51	.35	-.56
Format (Basics)	.30	.19	.28	.18

Discussion

The results provide mixed support for our peer-review practices in ENC1101 and ENC1102. On the one hand, it is encouraging to observe that students' reviews were more positively correlated with instructors' reviews over time, suggesting that either students and instructors are getting more adept at identifying quality writing or that students are getting a better sense of their instructor's preferences. These results echo the results of Liang and Tsai who found correlations between instructors and students improved over time on a four-point analytic scale, which suggests, not surprisingly perhaps, that practice improves peer reviews. Additionally, the finding that stronger writers, as identified by their instructors' grades on their papers, have scores more highly correlated with instructors and a broader variance in their scores than weaker students affirms peer-review pedagogy for more accomplished writers.

On the other hand, the difficulties students have distinguishing between B and C papers and the lack of variation in their ratings suggest there are problems with our peer-review practices. While the discrepancy between student and instructor scores, particularly those reviews conducted by students who do not receive high grades for writing assignments, suggests instructors and students need to be skeptical of students' numeric evaluations of other students' work, the finding that peer reviews of students become more highly correlated with instructors over time suggests that there is some value to this practice. In addition, just because some students, particularly students who receive lower grades on their writing from instructors, may not be able to score like their instructors doesn't mean they aren't providing useful critical feedback or that going through this process isn't helpful in terms of helping them better understand their instructor's grading criteria or academic conventions for writing well.

Before assuming the lack of agreements between instructors and students invariably undermines the validity of peer review in general, we need to research the lexical comments peers provide one another. It could be that social pressures warrant inflated grades, yet the sticky notes, rubric dialog boxes, community comments, and endnotes may provide more critical, useful feedback. To research this point in the future, we are currently text mining students' comments and instructors from a lexical perspective. We are also working with colleagues at Malmö University in Sweden and University of Tartu in Estonia to look at cultural differences in peer reviews. Beyond conducting a lexical analysis of comments offered by peer reviewers and instructors at different university writing programs, we believe we need to measure the effects of comments and scores on revision before determining whether or not a discuss rubric is invariably superior to a numeric rubric. Alternatively, given that we found students and instructors may fixate on an overall value of a work being rated and then apply that holistic score to whatever sub-criteria are defined by a rubric, it could be that the psychology of assigning numbers in a column in this way creates a tendency to the mean because of an anchoring effect (Englich, Mussweiler, and Strack). If so, this argues that we should be more thoughtful about how rubric scales are constructed and what they are supposed to measure. Since conducting this study, we have modified My Reviewers to allow for more variation in rubrics and rubric scales.

Our results differ from those of Cho and Schunn, as well as Cho, Chung, King, and Schunn, who found that students found peer reviews superior to instructor reviews when at least six students conducted the reviews. Our results in this study, our analysis of teacher commentary (Dixon and Moxley), and our analysis of 52,001 essays scored by instructors in our program (Tackitt, Moxley, and Eubanks) do not support Cho et al.'s argument that instructors' expert status prevents them from providing the detailed, contextualized feedback students need and that they are likely to underestimate the difficulty of revising. Perhaps this is due to a difference in context: We were working with English faculty while Cho et al. were working with STEM faculty. While possible, these disciplinary distinctions may not explain our divergent findings, so we would like to pursue this question in the future: thanks to USF funding, we are now examining peer review in STEM courses at USF, University of Pennsylvania, MIT, Dartmouth, and NCSU. Once this corpus develops, we will compare students' peer review experiences in STEM courses as well as English courses.

Because of this analysis of 46,689 student and instructor reviews of intermediate drafts and those of a related study that analyzes 52,001 scores provided by instructors on intermediate and final drafts (Tackitt et al.), we decided it was time to change the rubrics we use in first-year composition. As discussed above, the finding that a sizable percentage of any click was a holistic score suggested to us that we were asking our instructors and students to click too many criteria. While we stand by our earlier accounts regarding the surprising benefits of using a community rubric across genres and sections of ENC1101 and ENC1102 (see Moxley "Big Data"), beginning in the fall 2015 semester we have implemented genre-specific rubrics for our three projects in both courses. In the newest iteration of My Reviewers, we have accounted for all possible permutations: Administrators may now standardize rubric(s) across a program; alternatively, instructors may create rubrics with unlimited criteria. Administrators and instructors may now customize the scoring scale, dynamically adding as many milestones as they wish, with a minimum of two points and a maximum of 100 points (see fig. 5), and they can click on any part of the sliding scale to make more nuanced scoring determinations.

Despite this and related research, we remain somewhat conflicted regarding best peer review and writing program assessment practices. Not surprisingly, perhaps, we find ourselves oscillating between two dominant approaches to assessment: a modernist view that reifies grading and a postmodern view that embraces subjective responses to students' works. Of course, we are well aware of limitations with the modernist view, which assumes that descriptions of levels of achievement, combined with a system for collecting data, will produce ratings that correspond to the reified categories. Clearly, for example, the assumption that students (or instructors) will weigh the use of evidence in a piece of writing and produce a rating that corresponds to that (reified) construct overlooks legitimate differences in kinds and degrees of evidence needed by different readers or audiences. We understand that standardized assessments that are based in inauthentic,

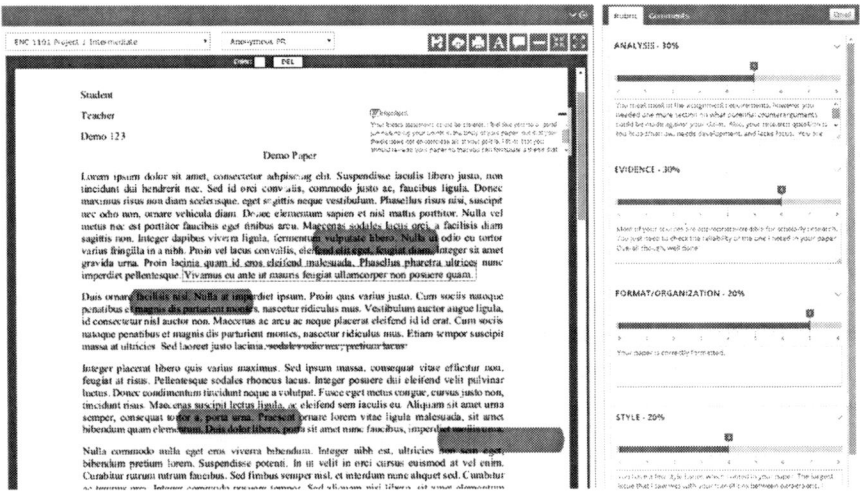

Fig. 5. Sample discuss rubric template.

out-of-class assignments and that strip texts from contexts may result in disingenuous, harmful claims. We understand that contemporary assessment practices are invariably racist and that students in the bottom quartile of the class struggle to improve against a headwind of negative feedback. We understand traditional rubrics have tended to focus on cognitive measures as opposed to addressing intrapersonal and interpersonal competencies.

Ultimately, however, society keeps score. Teachers, college admissions officers, accrediting bodies, legislators, employers, and governments all keep score. Instructors are required to provide grades. We know, for example, that the College Board determined in 2013 that 57% of SAT takers do not qualify as college ready ("2013 SAT Report" 3); that the ACT found 31% of high school graduates "did not meet any of the ACT College Readiness Benchmarks" ("The Condition of College" 4); that the NAEP Writing Report found 73% of 12th graders received scores of Below Basic or Basic as opposed to Proficient or Advanced in 2011 (National Center for Education Statistics); that the US literacy rate fell from 10th to 20th in the latest study on global rankings, Programme for International Student Assessment 2012 (PISA 2012). Clearly, these assessments have economic consequences. When it comes to employment, it matters that Blacks and Hispanics score significantly lower than whites on tests such as the NAEP assessment of writing. Moving forward, we are committed to further exploring how we can develop Writing Analytics at My Reviewers to identify data patterns for administrators, instructors, and students that can be used to improve peer review practices. We question how Writing Analytics, which repurpose data in the system (user trace patterns, lexical comments, scores, survey responses) can help writers and reviewers navigate the middle ground between extreme subjective or objective views of assessment. One possible approach is suggested by so-called non-cognitive measures, where we do not solely focus on isolated products of student work as proxies for some platonic student ability, but treat attitudes, beliefs, and behaviors related to writing as equally important. This greatly broadens the potential for meaningful assessment and pedagogy that impacts students in new ways.

Future Research

We believe a richer portrait of peer-review processes needs to be developed, one that accounts for students' and instructors' written comments and the effects of these comments on subsequent drafts, and one that accounts for lexical comments as associated with particular user attitudes, beliefs, and behaviors. We need lexical, descriptive work on what instructors and students are saying to one another and how these comments and scores support writing development. After all, students' comments on one another's papers may have a profound effect on the development of students' intrapersonal, interpersonal, and cognitive competencies. While a grade provides students information regarding the quality of their work in relation to their peers, students need thoughtful in-text and endnote comments to improve as writers.

Beyond employing sentiment analysis of the lexical corpus, future studies need to examine if a large set of students and instructors from different schools and different backgrounds will provide the same or similar results. We believe it would be especially helpful to evaluate how particular cohorts perform, such as students with high GPA or AP English scores or students from an L2 background. We also think it would be useful to study the response styles of instructor groups by disciplinary lens, such as literature versus creative writing versus Professional and Technical Writing versus Rhetoric and Composition. Perhaps the permissions at My Reviewers should permit students to see other students' scoring and markup as well as the instructors' scoring and markup—absent the instructor's grades, given FERPA—after the instructor grades peer review efforts.

Furthermore, we need experimental work that develops and tests algorithms and workflows. As symbol analysts, tool developers, and writing program administrators embedded in writing programs, we wonder what information digital tools such as My Reviewers can provide to facilitate better reviews, writing development, and transfer of cognitive, intrapersonal, and interpersonal competencies.

Notes

1. Professor Moxley wishes to disclose a potential conflict of interest. While the My Reviewers software is not commercially available, it may become commercially available in the future. Because the data collection methods used in this study demonstrate the viability of My Reviewers, this research study may enhance the commercial value of My Reviewers. Ultimately, USF owns My Reviewers; however, Moxley possesses the rights to license My Reviewers. Professor Moxley has filed the necessary USF conflict of interest paperwork. The Conflict of Interest Committee at USF has developed a management plan with which Dr. Moxley has complied prior to submitting this and similar research.

2. Following the 2009–2010 academic year, 10 independent scorers reviewed the third/final drafts of 249 students' essays in ENC1101 and 249 essays in ENC1102. In other words, the same 249 students were tracked for a year, and their essays for Project 2 in ENC1101 were compared with their essays for Project 2 in ENC1102. The independent evaluators were unaware of the students' identities, unaware of the students' instructors' identities, and unaware of the scores provided by the students' classroom instructors. A comparison between the two external evaluators and the students' classroom instructor revealed few differences between the classroom instructors and independent scorers on 7 of the 8 rubric measures. The only discrepancy between the instructors and the outside evaluators was the Style/Basics subcategory: On that measure, the students' classroom instructors were tougher in their judgments—about a third of a grade tougher.

3. It is interesting to note that in *Agency in the Age of Peer Production*, the qualitative study that historizes our effort to crowdsource our curriculum from a datagogical lens, we chronicle instructor resistance to a generic rubric. Now, when we introduced the idea of changing the generic rubric, for making rubrics distinct for each project, we experienced resistance. USF had been praised by the Southern Association of Colleges of Schools Commission on Colleges during its accreditation review, and the Office of Institutional Effectiveness, which had partnered with us in the crowdsourcing effort to develop the rubric, was happy with the rubric. After numerous years of using one rubric to assess across genres and sections of ENC1101 and ENC1102, instructors had grown accustomed to and comfortable with our rubric. When we initially suggested changing the rubric again, we sensed that people hoped we would leave well enough alone. To us, this suggests instructors derive benefits from a stable curriculum over time.

4. When instructors establish their peer review groups, they can choose between a discuss version and a numeric version of the rubric. The discuss version provides dialog spaces with grades, and the numeric version provides dialog boxes and grades. The default view is the numeric version.

5. Excluding book collections and conference proceedings, journals include *Assessment & Evaluation in Higher Education*, *British Educational Research Journal*, *Assessing Writing*, *Turkish Online Journal of Educational Technology*, *Issues in Education Research*, *Active Learning in Higher Education*, *International Journal for the*

Scholarship of Learning and Teaching, Journal of Writing Research, British Journal of Educational Technology, British Educational Research Journal, Instructional Science, The Internet and Higher Education, Journal of Educational Technology and Society, Journal of Second Language Writing, Computers and Education, Studies in Higher Education, Language Teaching Research, Journal of Second Language Writing, Review of Educational Research, and *Internet and Higher Education.*

6. Thanks to the recent development of corpus-based methods to record and analyze students' assessments, new methodologies now enable researchers to analyze large-scale studies of students' evaluations and teachers' comments. Rather than base results on small sample sizes, typically 5% of the population, the entire population can be researched. The behaviors of the population in a digital environment can also be passively recorded and researched within the limits of user agreements. Given all data is provided in real-time, digital tools shatter the traditional bifurcation of formative from summative evaluations.

7. The Community Comments are extensive, and we provide them in a book-length etext format as well as in the database format. Each Community Comment is a clickable hyperlink that leads to a resource page that defines the comment in an article and video and then gives students an opportunity to test their comprehension via an online quiz. A typical resource page includes the following sections pertaining to the topic: definition, identification, revision, common types, usage conventions, videos, activities, and external links. Most of the existing Community Comments address composition matters, but we are working with STEM faculty across the disciplines at USF, NCSU, MIT, Dartmouth, and Penn to build comments for other communities.

8. During the time of this study, the instructors who graded peer reviews assigned A grades 85% percent of the time. Many instructors ignored the policy requirement to grade peer reviews. The writing program administrators chose not to strictly enforce the policy that peer reviews should be graded by instructors because they have chosen to adopt a soft power approach as outlined in *Agency in the Age of Peer Production.*

9. At the time of this study, we did not have IRB approval to match demographic data to user behaviors. We have since received that permission and are working on additional studies that maps behaviors by demographics and other variables, including grit, self-efficacy, and self-regulation.

Works Cited

ACT. "The Condition of College & Career Readiness 2013." *ACT* (2013): 1–32. Web. 8 Feb. 2016.

Anson, Chris M., Deanna P. Dannels, Pamela Flash, and Amy L. Housley Gaffney. "Big Rubrics and Weird Genres: The Futility of Using Generic Assessment Tools Across Diverse Instructional Contexts." *Journal of Writing Assessment* 5.1 (2012): n. pag. Web. 13 Mar. 2016.

Anson, Chris, Joseph Moxley, Djuddah Leijen, Damian Finnegan, Anna Wärnsby, and Asko Kauppinen. "Theorizing Community Rubrics: Limits, Research, and Case Studies." *8th Biennial Conference of the European Association for the Teaching of Academic Writing.* Tallinn University of Technology, Estonia. 15–17 June 2015. Presentation.

Boase-Jelinek, Daniel, Jenni Parker, and Jan Herrington. "Student Reflection and Learning through Peer Reviews." *Teaching and Learning in Higher Education: Western Australia's TL Forum.* Spec. issue of *Issues in Educational Research* 23.2 (2013): 119–31. Print.

Cho, Kwangsu, Tingting Rachel Chung, William R. King, and Christian Schunn. "Peer-Based Computer-Supported Knowledge Refinement: An Empirical Investigation." *Communications of the ACM* 51.3 (2008): 83–88. Print.

Cho, Kwangsu, and Christian D. Schunn. "Scaffolded Writing and Rewriting in the Discipline: A Web-Based Reciprocal Peer Review System." *Computers & Education* 48.3 (2005): 409–26. Print.

College Board. "2013 SAT Report on College and Career Readiness." *College Board* (2013): 1–9. Web. 8 Feb. 2016.

Crossman, Joanne M., and Stacey L. Kite. "Facilitating Improved Writing among Students through Directed Peer Review." *Active Learning in Higher Education* 13.3 (2012): 219–29. Print.

Dixon, Zachary, and Joseph Moxley. "Everything Is Illuminated: What Big Data Can Tell Us about Teacher Commentary." *Assessing Writing* 18.4 (2013): 241–56. Web. 13 Mar. 2016.

Englich, Birte, Thomas Mussweiler, and Fritz Strack. "Playing Dice with Criminal Sentences: The Influence of Irrelevant Anchors on Experts' Judicial Decision Making." *Personality and Social Psychology Bulletin* 32.2 (2006): 188–200. Print.

Esfandiari, Rajab, and Carol M. Myford. "Severity Differences Among Self-assessors, Peer-assessors, and Teacher Assessors Rating EFL Essays." *Assessing Writing* 8.2 (2013): 111–31. Print.

Eubanks, David. "A Geometric Approach to Conditional Inter-Rater Agreement." 2015. TS. Furman University, South Carolina.

Falchikov, Nancy, and David Boud. "Student Self-Assessment in Higher Education: A Meta-Analysis." *Review of Educational Research* 59.4 (1989): 395–430. Print.

Falchikov, Nancy, and Douglas Magin. "Detecting Gender Bias in Peer Marking of Students' Group Process Work." *Assessment & Evaluation in Higher Education* 22.4 (1997): 385–96. Print.

Falchikov, Nancy, and Judy Goldfinch. "Student Peer Assessment in Higher Education: A Meta-Analysis Comparing Peer and Teacher Marks." *Review of Educational Research* 70.3 (2000): 287–322. Print.

Haswell, Richard H. "NCTE/CCCC's Recent War on Scholarship." *Written Communication* 22.2 (2005): 198–223. Print.

Khonbi, Zainab Abolfazli, and Karim Sadeghi. "The Effect of Assessment Type (Self Vs. Peer) on Iranian University EFL Students' Course Achievement." *Procedia-Social and Behavioral Sciences* 70 (2013): 1552–64. Print.

Langbehn, Karen, Megan McIntyre, and Joe M. Moxley. "Re-Mediating Writing Program Assessment." *Digital Writing Assessment & Evaluation*. Ed. Heidi McKee and Dànielle Nicole DeVoss. Logan: Computers and Composition Digital Press, n. pag. Web. 13 Mar. 2016.

Li, Lan, Liu Xiongyi, and Yuchun Zhou. "Give and Take: A Re-Analysis of Assessor and Assessee's Roles in Technology-Facilitated Peer Assessment." *British Journal of Educational Technology* 43.3 (2012): 376–84. Web. 13 Feb. 2016.

Liang, Jyh-Chong, and Chin-Chung Tsai. "Learning through Science Writing via Online Peer Assessment in a College Biology Course." *The Internet and Higher Education* 13.4 (2010): 242–47. Print.

Liu, Eric Zhi-Feng, and Chun-Yi Lee. "Using Peer Feedback to Improve Learning via Online Peer Assessment." *Turkish Online Journal of Educational Technology* 12.1 (2013): 187–99. Print.

Liu, Xiongyi, and Lan Li. "Assessment Training Effects on Student Assessment Skills and Task Performance in a Technology-Facilitated Peer Assessment." *Assessment & Evaluation in Higher Education* 39.3 (2014): 275–92. Print.

Lu, Yingjie, Pengzhu Zhang, Jingfang Liu, Jia Li, and Shasha Deng. "Health-Related Hot Topic Detection in Online Communities Using Text Clustering." *PLoS ONE* 8.2 (2013): n. pag. Web. 13 Feb. 2016.

Lundstrom, Kristi, and Wendy Baker. "To Give Is Better Than to Receive: The Benefits of Peer Review to the Reviewer's Own Writing." *Journal of Second Language Writing* 18.1 (2009): 30–43. Print.

Moxley, Joseph M. "Aggregated Assessment and 'Objectivity 2.0.'" *Proceedings of the Second Workshop on Computational Linguistics and Writing (CLW 2012): Linguistic and Cognitive Aspects of Document Creation and Document Engineering*. 23 Apr. 2012: 19–26. Web. 13 March 2016.

—. "Big Data, Learning Analytics, and Social Assessment." *Journal of Writing Assessment* 6.1 (2013): n. pag. Web. 13 Feb. 2016.

National Center for Education Statistics. "The Nation's Report Card: Writing 2011." *National Center for Education Statistics*. Institute of Education Sciences, US Department of Education, Washington, DC. Sept. 2012. Web. 8 Feb. 2016.

Patchan, Melissa M., Christian D. Schunn, and Russell J. Clark. "Writing in Natural Sciences: Understanding the Effects of Different Types of Reviewers on the Writing Process." *Journal of Writing Research* 2.3 (2011): 365–93. Print.

Programme for International Student Assessment. "Programme for International Student Assessment (PISA) Results from PISA 2012: United States." *OECD*. PISA, n.d. Web. 8 Feb. 2016.

Schneider, Barbara, Martin Carnoy, Jeremy Kilpatrick, William H. Schmidt, and Richard J. Shavelson. *Estimating Causal Effects: Using Experimental and Observational Designs*. Washington, DC: American Educational Research Association, 2007. Print.

Tackitt, Alaina, Joe M. Moxley, and David Eubanks. "Big Rubrics and Big Data: The Development, Transfer, Prediction, and Restriction of Student Competencies." 2015. TS. *Assessing Writing*.

Takeda, Sachiko, and Fabian Homberg. "The Effects of Gender on Group Work Process and Achievement: An Analysis through Self- and Peer-Assessment." *British Educational Research Journal* 40.2 (2014): 373–96. Print.

Topping, Keith J. "Peers as a Source of Formative and Summative Assessment." *SAGE Handbook of Research on Classroom Assessment*. Ed. James H. McMillan. Thousand Oaks: SAGE, 2012. Print.

—. "Peer Assessment between Students in Colleges and Universities." *Review of Educational Research* 68.3 (1998): 249–76. Print.

Topping, Keith J., Elaine F. Smith, Ian Swanson, and Audrey Elliot. "Formative Peer Assessment of Academic Writing between Postgraduate Students." *Assessment and Evaluation in Higher Education* 25.2 (2000): 149–69. Print.

Tucker, Richard. "Sex Does Not Matter: Gender Bias and Gender Differences in Peer Assessments of Contributions to Group Work." *Assessment & Evaluation in Higher Education* 39.3 (2014): 293–309. Print.

Vierrege, Quentin D., Kyle D. Stedman, Taylor Joy Mitchell, and Joseph M. Moxley. *Agency in the Age of Peer Production*. Urbana: NCTE, 2012. Print.

ACKNOWLEDGMENTS

We thank Norbert Elliot for his critical feedback and encouragement on this article. For their vigorous editorial work article on this article, we thank Barbara L'Eplattenier, Lisa Mastrangelo, Sherry Rankins-Robertson, and Davee Sarim. Finally, we thank Val Ross who has played a critical role in the on-going development of My Reviewers. This research is supported by the National Science Foundation under Award #1544239, "Collaborative Research: The Role of Instructor and Peer Feedback in Improving the Cognitive, Interpersonal, and Intrapersonal Competencies of Student Writers in STEM Courses."

Joseph M. Moxley <http://joemoxley.org> is the founder of Writing Commons *<http://writingcommons.org>, a free alternative to expensive writing textbooks. Peer-reviewed,* Writing Commons *provides open access to over 1,000 webtexts, making it a viable choice as the required textbook for composition, professional and technical writing, creative nonfiction, and creative writing courses. Moxley is also Director of First-Year Composition at the University of South Florida, a Research 1 university.*

David Eubanks is Assistant Vice President for Assessment and Institutional Effectiveness at Furman University, a private liberal arts university.

Taming Big Data through Agile Approaches to Instructor Training and Assessment: Managing Ongoing Professional Development in Large First-Year Writing Programs

Susan M. Lang

Abstract

This piece responds to Donna Strickland's call in The Managerial Unconscious *in that it embraces and examines the idea of managerial work through the use of tools and practices previously unavailable. Indeed, the practices discussed in this article exemplify the idea that the intellectual work of the WPA can and should contain a substantial managerial component in order to most effectively assist instructors and students. When one focuses on central components of a WPA's work, such as training new instructors to comment on student work, merging the intellectual and the managerial is critical to conduct training in the most helpful ways. An increasing number of writing programs are incorporating databases, course and learning management software, and/or digital submission of writing into their routines. As instructors digitally respond to students' writing by using these technologies, emerging concepts and practices previously more commonly associated with information technology—concepts such as big data and agile—may help administrators, instructors, and students have more productive experiences in their writing programs. These concepts, along with the emerging methodologies of data and text mining, can enable administrators to work closely with instructors to assess instruction and solve issues that surface as quickly and as effectively as possible.*

As an increasing number of writing programs incorporate databases, course and learning management software, and/or digital submission of writing into their routines, and as instructors digitally respond to student writing, emerging practices previously more commonly associated with information technology—practices such as big data and agile[1]—may help administrators to ensure that both instructors and students have more productive experiences in their writing programs. Indeed, data-driven approaches to teaching and assessment and agile approaches to change were named as two of the six "key trends . . . that are likely to enter mainstream use" within the next five years in *The New Media Horizon Report: 2014 Higher Education Edition*. These two trends, along with online, hybrid, and collaborative learning (also discussed in the same report) promise change for many parts of higher education. Yet, as the US Department of Education's 2012 *Enhancing Teaching and Learning through Educational Data Mining and Learning Analytics* recommends:

> Educators need to experience having student data that tell them something useful and actionable about teaching and learning. This means that instructors must have near-real-time access to easy-to-understand visual representations of student learning data at a level of detail that can inform their instructional decisions. . . . The kinds of data provided to instructors need to be truly helpful in making instructional decisions, and instructors will need to come to these learning data with a different mind-set than that engendered by data systems geared to serving purposes of accountability. (46)

The report also discusses areas throughout higher education where these tools can make a difference. While writing programs and writing instruction are not mentioned specifically in these reports, there are clearly places in our work where these technologies and processes can make significant impacts. The useful and actionable data referred to above enables us to explore and potentially answer such questions as the following:

- What do students do when faced with a particular rhetorical challenge in a writing course?
- How do new instructors compare to their more experienced counterparts when it comes to responding to student writing?
- How do students respond to commentary that seems too brief? Too lengthy? Too vague? And what are the key indicators of the students' responses?

At its most elemental, then, the term *big data* describes datasets too large and complex to handle by conventional methods.[2] While the sheer number of artifacts (student assignments, comments on those assignments, grades) associated with writing programs certainly don't approach the millions of data points accumulated in other enterprises, examining even several hundred or several thousand documents on a regular basis, has been beyond the abilities of WPAs until recently. The term *agile* refers to a rapid and occasionally chaotic type of project management most commonly associated with software development. Although the principles behind agile management are expanding beyond software, the idea of rapid response is not something ordinarily associated with higher education or writing instruction. Instead, big data and agile methods are heavily intertwined with technology and with quantitative data use—items that until recently were not a typical part of many WPAs' daily consciousness. Integrating both, however, into a program's organizational framework enables WPAs to conduct effective and accelerated instructor evaluation (or assessment) so that managed change can occur within the current semester, in addition to being phased in over subsequent semesters. For example, big data has been specifically referenced by Moxley in the context of understanding student learning. Likewise, the University of Georgia's <emma>, an electronic markup and documentation management application, has been used for nearly a decade now as both "essay processor and database" (Barrett et al. 37) and enabled a recent study of over 5,000 citations in student essays. Langbehn, McIntyre, and Moxley discuss the importance of real-time study and response (a.k.a., agile) in understanding what modifications might be needed in a writing program curriculum. In our first-year writing program, both big data and agile have played increasingly integral roles for the past several years. In this article, I'll discuss how the program has leveraged big data and agile practices, along with more traditional methods, to improve our professional development program for our graduate instructors by gaining a better understanding of the behaviors of its various stakeholders.

With the help of both qualitative and quantitative data, I break down traditional timelines as I work with instructors to support classroom/pedagogical and assessment practices. I and my associate director do so in many ways—through frequent meetings among instructor groups, more formal workshops, and individual meetings with instructors. In addition, I use our in-house software, the Raider Writer application, as well as commercial text and data mining software to help identify topics of discussion, areas of strengths and weakness in instructors' responses to students, and other items that help ensure that the program meets the needs of both the first-year students and our instructors. As Shirley K Rose suggests, those of us in composition studies "must understand our scholarly role as organizers employing strategic rhetoric to engage our institutions and communities in effecting change and to reflect on our actions" (230); in this first-year writing program, engagement and reflection may start with a single instructor or single student's assignment and strategically scale up to comprehensive and longitudinal program views.

A Bit of External Context

In their 2011 *WPA: Writing Program Administration* article, Taggart and Lowery note that "teacher preparation should not end when the [graduate teacher preparation] course is over; rather, TAs' professional development as teachers continues until they graduate" (106). Indeed, much of the discussion for the last two decades regarding TA preparation for teaching first-year writing has focused on the particulars of the initial preparation course—the common element in nearly every program charged with training graduate students in the teaching of first-year writing—or other reflective or mentoring exercises that become part of the first or second semester of teaching. Until recently, far less attention has been paid to what WPAs can do to conduct meaningful and ongoing training, mentoring, and evaluating of these instructors beyond the initial semester, especially those practices that can be implemented before a graduate instructor graduates or moves on to another course. Estrem and Reid's "Writing Pedagogy Education" notes that scholarship on writing pedagogy education (WPE) should incorporate a more "systematic research" approach to complement the "thoughtful lore" that encompasses much of the field and examine training "well beyond the TA seminar" (224). Specifically, they argue for more long-term analysis informed by data "of the ways in which preservice, inservice, and continuing service WPE interact and reinforce one another" (238–39). Obermark, Brewer, and Halasek's "Moving from the One and Done to a Culture of Collaboration: Revising Professional Development for TAs" calls for an ongoing professional development program, one that responds to changing needs of graduate instructors as they move through their various teaching assignments.

One such area that requires further study is how WPAs effectively conduct timely and ongoing evaluation of our graduate instructors. Diana Ashe notes that

> While our classes are taught by an assemblage that changes radically each semester, we cannot pretend to make many claims about the consistency of the quality of our teachers. This is not to say that we do not have wonderful and dedicated teachers; it would seem from all of the available, anecdotal evidence that the contrary is true. The problem here is clear: we can have only anecdotal evidence to rely upon while we depend on a heavily contingent workforce. (156–67)

Ashe calls for diachronic forms of evaluation and assessment to supplement the more synchronic forms, such as student evaluations or classroom observations. Both synchronic tools have their limitations in programs where a significant number of instructors average only one or two semesters of teaching a particular course. Depending on the size of the program and administrators available to observe, instructors may only be observed once or twice annually with no allowance for follow-ups. Student evaluations have limited use to assist with professional development for a couple of reasons. First, in many programs, evaluations aren't available for viewing and analysis until several weeks into the following semester. Furthermore, many questions on traditional evaluation forms focus more on what is known as "satisfaction-based assessment" (Allen 97) in which students are asked their opinions about such topics as the ability of the instructor to "stimulate student learning" or to move "beyond presenting the information in the text." Occasionally, a question might ask students about their engagement or participation in the form of the number of hours they spend weekly on a course, but few if any of the questions on the forms ever require students to engage in a discussion of what they actually learned. In short, while student evaluation information regarding satisfaction and participation can provide important data, information from the evaluations doesn't help us close the loop and revise or refine our training and assessment practices.

Clearly, if WPAs want to provide ongoing training to their instructors, we need more current information to do so. One of the most immediate information sources comes from both instructor and student response to current curricular requirements. For example, in discussing the use of their My Reviewers peer review application, Langbehn, McIntyre, and Moxley note that

> By analyzing in real-time how students and teachers are responding to a curriculum, WPAs and teachers can work with one another to fine-tune assignments and crowdsource effective teacher feedback, thus improving program assessment results. Most significantly, because of the immediacy enabled by a digital system, they can accomplish this in real time as WPAs trace teacher responses and grades, as indicators of strengths and challenges, on a day-to-day basis. (n. pag)

How WPAs choose to view our training and assessment of instructors is a critical part of many programs that predominantly rely on a work force comprised of graduate students and contingent faculty.[3] While many may still object to any labeling of our work as managerial (and often fail to do more than stereotype and discount that term), Strickland's call for an "operative approach" (120) to program direction opens other possibilities. If operative management practices can serve as catalysts for action and leave "nothing off the table," (121) why not create professional development activities commensurate with the dynamic nature and large scale of first-year writing (or any writing program and many general education programs)? Given the ongoing nature of assessment now required by accrediting agencies, many of our programs need a different approach to instructor training and assessment, one that can accommodate a variety of training and assessment strategies, people, and timeframes—in short, programs need to become agile.

Applying Agile

Agile methods value many of the same things WPAs do: individuals, interactions, collaboration, and productive response to change. While created for software design projects, the philosophical elements of agile are being increasingly adopted for other situations that contain dynamic, time-sensitive, and unpredictable elements.[4] In academic settings, agile and other time-sensitive methods are gaining favor as tools for instructional and assessment programs and redesigns. Bradley discusses a model of assessment that, although less comprehensive, is carried out in a cycle of a few months to a year and creates opportunities to close the loop; he notes that "[w]ithin the next year, of our 26 departments, 15 had closed the loop for at least one assessment task and 6 additional departments had put structures in place for reviewing assessment data and responding to them" (11). Schwieger and Surendran describe their rationale for revising a single course using agile: "[agile's] test and evaluate principle, [sic] provides the underlying motivation behind its use. . . . The process of identifying small goals, collecting and processing data about the progress towards those goals, and then evaluating the progress and acting upon the evaluation results has been found to be beneficial in multiple capacities" (4). In "Agile Learning Design," Groves et al. describe how IBM came to adopt elements of agile for its learning design of employee training.[5] They conclude that "[w]ith agile, our emphasis is on enabling employees to learn immediately and leveraging their experiences to drive improvements into the continuously improving overall learning experience" (51). This immediacy is a critical component of professional development. For example, if an instructor has misunderstood an element of an assignment, having the resources available for her to review a key concept or to examine other instructors' responses to that same assignment may make the difference in the quality of her evaluation and feedback to her students. In the case of most large writing programs, both the students and the instructors will benefit from immediate opportunities to learn. Thus all involved have much to gain from administrative and instructional processes that can respond quickly to change.

Having It Both Ways—Developing Deliverables that Work and Valuing People over Processes

Our hybrid writing program has incorporated web-based, data-driven applications for well over a decade. In addition to distributing instruction between the classroom and the online environment, administrators distributed the responsibilities for teaching students between the brick and mortar classroom and online evaluation of student writing. Much of the early discussion regarding the program (Kemp, Wasley) dealt with the apparent benefits and liabilities of the distributed evaluation system. Originally, program administrators focused on creating and supporting interfaces for the distributed grading process. Thus, the initial phase of the model placed a premium on collecting data—whether that be student response to assignments or instructor commentary on those assignments. Far less attention was paid to how or if that data would be used to improve the user experience.

The user experience (instructor or student) demands more attention. In many large programs, instructors often seem isolated—they teach their own courses, grade their own students, and know very little beyond anecdotal evidence about what is happening in other sections of the courses they teach. Initially, our program of distributed assessment did little to remedy this. Some instructors were able to focus primarily on classroom teaching and face-to-face interactions with students, and others on responding to student assignments online, but because all assignments were pushed into a single course pool, little significant conversation occurred between classroom instructors and online graders about specific elements of assignments. Both types of instructors reported a continued sense of isolation, especially those whose teaching assignment was conducted primarily online.

I and my associate director have worked to remedy this, though, in the past seven years. Set up in groups at the beginning of the semester, four to six instructors collaborate to instruct 140–230 students during a semester. The variance in number of students and size of the groups is determined by the instructors' teaching/grading load. Some work for us for as little as 0.125 FTE, most work for either 0.25 or 0.50 FTE, and some work the equivalent of a full-time 4/4 load. Most appointments are split in some way between classroom instruction and grading, unless the instructor is a first-year MA or a PhD student who hasn't met SACS coursework requirements to be a teacher of record or has specifically requested that her entire appointment be as a grader. When at all possible, instructors of varying experience levels are grouped together to create a built-in mentoring system and knowledge base about the program.

To complement this knowledge base, I've made a conscious and determined effort to provide instructors with data that facilitates communication among them and enables a degree of self-assessment in addition to the more traditional, administratively initiated discussions. In retrospect, this evolution speaks to the first five of Marschall's adapted tenets. The program often delivers new features in software, as well as in the overall professional development program, and upgrades those features frequently as administrators develop improvements. While I am sensitive to the potential downside of introducing a new feature during a semester, especially with new users involved, administrators work closely with those instructors and students to bring elements online that enhance their experience. Additionally, I enable instructors to play to their strengths or needs: Those who thrive in the classroom often take on more sections, but commensurately less grading, and those who need to live or work away from campus take on grading-only assignments. Given the flexible nature of the program's teaching assignments, instructors who wish to increase their competency in a particular area of their teaching can also do so. However, with this increased dispersion comes a greater need for community and communication. Nowhere is this more apparent than in discussion of student assignments and instructor responses to assignments.

For over 30 years, scholars have examined the nature and role of commentary on student assignments. Since Sommers and Brannon and Knoblauch initiated the contemporary discussion in 1982, studies have ranged from the large (Lunsford and Connors' "Teachers' Rhetorical Comments on Student Papers" and Smith's "The Genre of the End Comment") to the fine-grained (Batt's "The Rhetoric of the End Comment"). Regardless of the size of the study, all echo the thoughts of Rick Straub:

> More than the general principles we voice or the theoretical approach we take into the class, it is what we value in student writing, how we communicate those values, and what we say individually on student texts that carry the most weight in writing instruction. It is how we receive and respond to the words students put on the page that speaks loudest in our teaching. (246)

Despite the importance of the comment, both Batt and Smith remind readers that specifics of the written comment generally aren't taught in teacher-training programs, and Smith notes that instructors "rarely share their comments with each other" (249). She continues with some observations about the temporality of the comments, noting that "[e]nd comments are not preserved in one location for perusal by members of the community. Teachers rarely read their comments more than once or twice, since comments are widely dispersed shortly after they are written" (249). The transient nature of these critical comments has previously made their study difficult, as first Lunsford and Connors, and later Lunsford and Lunsford, found as they described their attempts to collect commented-upon papers. When considering the context of the comment in a larger context—that in which new TAs learn to teach—the importance of repeated opportunities to discuss and reflect on these comments becomes even more critical.[6] Reid, Estrem, and Belcheir, in discussing their "newly intensified understanding of the pedagogy learning process as lengthy, initially partial, and recursive," (59) recommend that programs must provide "regular, formal, directed pedagogy education" beyond the first year to have any substantial impact (61). They also recommend reflective practice throughout a TA's time in the program.

The ability to store and analyze instructor commentary on student assignments, particularly in the context of those assignments, would hold significant promise for furthering the study of instructor commentary even if such analysis could only occur at the conclusion of a semester's teaching. However, the ability of text mining software to enable reflective analysis at various points (weekly or after particular assignments have been evaluated) and of various magnitudes (for a single instructor, for a single grading group, or for a particular demographic of students or instructors) during a semester can help create a more immediate impact for instructors and students alike. Still an emerging field, text mining draws upon fields as diverse as library and information science, computational linguistics, statistics, artificial intelligence, and machine learning in a quest to analyze and process semistructured and unstructured text data. Text mining brings together qualitative and quantitative methodologies to discover knowledge in a corpus of texts; it is a largely exploratory process with the goal of extracting meaning from texts. In the case of such software packages as QDA Miner, modules such as Word Stat, the text mining component, provide quantitative compliments to the main QDA Miner, which enables content analysis of a corpus of texts. What is key here is that the technology enables textual analysis by WPAs and instructors on scales heretofore impossible in a timeframe capable of improving the experiences of both current students and instructors.[7]

Using the Data

Our Raider Writer software, like any LMS such as BlackBoard or D2L, records every grade assigned by an instructor to every assignment, along with the commentary provided for the student. The data is exported into Excel or to QDA Miner and can then be filtered by course, course section, grading workgroup section, assignment type, individual assignment, or individual instructor. These components are examined individually, in combination, and in the context of the student writing to which they respond, using both descriptive statistics and rhetorical and content analysis. Since both instructors and administrators have access to qualitative and quantitative data concerning their commentary and grades,[8] assessment is initiated by both parties throughout a semester. For example, each semester an instructor works in the program, her comments for that semester are stored and remain accessible to her. She can review these at any time to remind herself of effective strategies for responding to particular assignments or compare any changes in the way she responds to an assignment. For instructors in their first or second year in the program, this element can help resolve questions for themselves and other group members about any number of aspects of responding to student work by breaking down traditional temporal boundaries.

Access to this data enables instructors to become, in some respects, the self-organizing teams that are a principle component of agile methods. All instructors in a grading group have access to the assignments, comments, and grades of the students in their courses.[9] All instructors are encouraged to review their own and other group members' average grades for each assignment, as well as recent comments made by their group members on assignments. Classroom instructors review comments and grades for their sections, both in the context of class preparation each week or at individual student requests. These reviews often prompt an instructor to contact an administrator to discuss a range of questions, which may include requests to evaluate the effectiveness of their own comments, explain the difference in strategies between their work and that of their colleagues, or to discuss differences in numerical grades assigned on work that is apparently similar in quality. In addition, though, through our web interface, administrators can evaluate comments and grades on assignments after an instructor has graded only a few of each assignment and offer suggestions that can be applied while the instructor grades the rest of her assigned drafts or before any brief follow-up is scheduled (Marschall's 6th tenet). One of the principle advantages of these intervention strategies is that the instructors have time to read, reflect, apply, and ask further questions at their convenience and/or while they are actually grading assignments. This process helps promote a sustainable environment, whereby instructors can continue their responding and assessing of student work without undue interruption (Marschall's 8th tenet). In exceptional cases, I can even return a commented assignment to an instructor for revision or expansion of their commentary so that improvement may occur for that instructor and that student within the semester.

Scaling Up: Text Mining Assignment Grades and Instructor Commentary

While evaluating individual comments allows a snapshot view of an instructor's work, I often want a larger field view of, say, 30 instructors' responses to a particular assignment or comments by one or more instructors on preliminary and final drafts of particular assignments. Elsewhere (Lang and Baehr 2012), I've discussed how text and data mining software enable program administrators to examine hundreds or thousands of documents from a variety of perspectives. I can view our students' and instructors' writing in ways that help communicate trends, strengths, and weaknesses in their work to both populations. I can look for patterns in grade distribution, on-time or late submissions of assignments, and number of assignments submitted—in a single semester or over several years—to prepare our instructors to assist students more effectively.

The following example uses 1,088 preliminary drafts of rhetorical analyses that were evaluated by instructors in either their first or second year in the program. This assignment was selected because it was the first time during the semester that instructors were asked to comment on a longer draft, and many new instructors had requested rapid feedback from us on their comments. Thus, I wanted to explore behaviors related to both commenting and assigning a numeric grade: what, specifically, were the first- and second-year instructors commenting on and if there appeared a reasonable correlation between the comments and the numeric grade assigned. Figure 1 shows the grade distribution for each of the 24 instructors under consideration.

View full-size images from this article using this QR code or online here: http://bit.ly/1U6t816

Fig. 1. Distribution of grades on preliminary drafts by instructor.

Several items become evident after examining this grid:

- The grades of 67 and 70 were the most frequently assigned, the former 53 times and the latter 48.
- Four graders (15329, 18436, 18445 and 18450) assigned more grades in the range 0–50 than the others.
- Mid-B to A grades were assigned approximately 12% of the time; second year students (identifiable by year through their IDs) tended to assign those more frequently.

Although all three of these observations could be explored in more detail, one stood out. The number of grades in the high-D range likely indicated that students were not writing a competent rhetorical analysis. If so, the comments written by instructors on those drafts, then, would be a critical component of whether or not those students could successfully revise those drafts and complete the course with the target grade of C or better. Another possibility is that instructors were struggling with their own comments on the drafts and correlating a grade accordingly. The 53 essays that were assigned a 67 were selected for examination, and the instructor comments filtered for closer study. Figure 2, below, shows the initial set of results—instructors inserted 506 comments in the 53 essays, from single words to detailed holistic comments. Clicking on any of these comments and then clicking on the window behind enables me to see the comment in context.

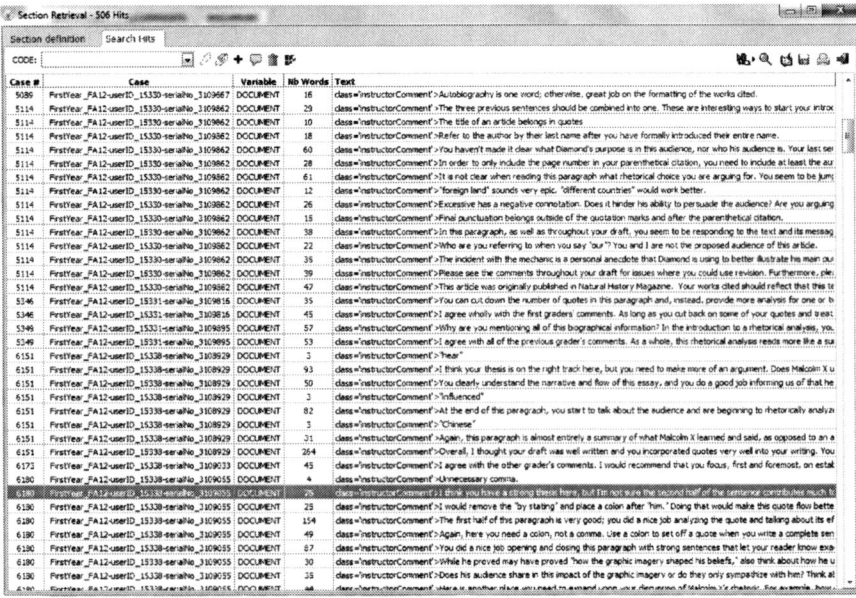

Fig. 2. Filtered instructor comments.

In order to examine more carefully the instructors' commenting behavior, I ran the Word Stat section of the software on these comments. I first examine word frequencies in the comments, represented by figure 3.

Fig. 3. Word frequencies.

From this screen, I can see that instructors most frequently used the terms *audience*, *rhetorical*, and *purpose* in their comments—over 20% of the comments written to students included one or more of those terms. Other words on this list would make it appear that instructors are most often discussing structural issues with students. However, to understand more of what is happening, I need to examine phrases and words in context. I am first able to pull more frequently used phrases (see fig. 4) While I obtain more evidence that instructors are discussing higher-level concerns with students, it's difficult to tell from them how much instruction is going on to help students with a text that they will be revising. One further step is required—to examine these words in context.

View full-size images from this article using this QR code or online here: http://bit.ly/1U6t816

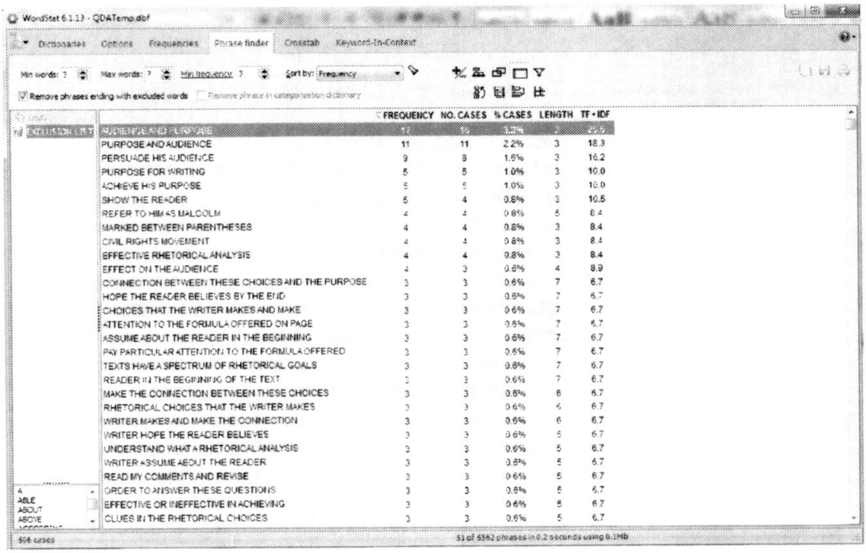

Fig 4. Phrase finder.

After selecting a particular term (*rhetorical*, in this case) and determining the amount of surrounding text to view, I can scroll through the various comments (see fig. 5) and see the highlighted word in context at the bottom of the page. I can quickly sample these and determine how instructors are using the term, as well as what type of instruction they are providing for the student.

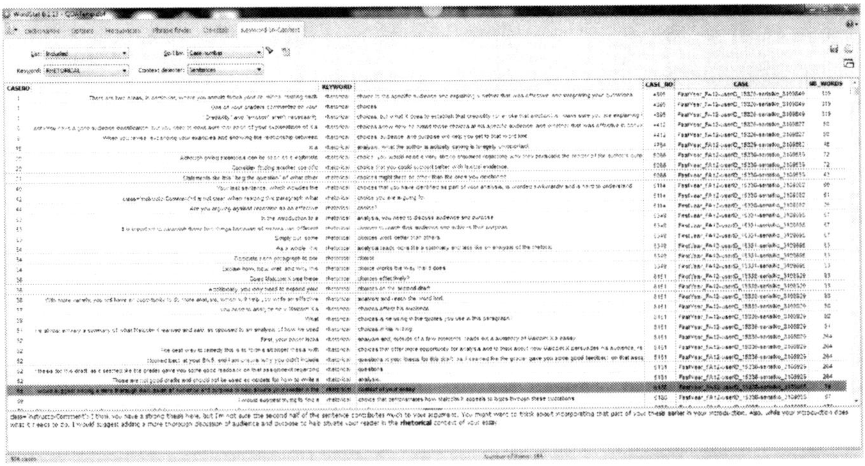

Fig. 5. Keyword in context.

I notice several trends that call for intervention. In the three comments quoted here, I see that all of them focus on either evaluation of a portion (or all) of the text and/or offer some suggestions for revision of the draft. The first two, in particular, exemplify Sommers' finding that "comments are not anchored in the particulars of the students' texts, but rather are a series of vague directives that are not text-specific" (153). This type of comment is one I see repeatedly in the work of new instructors. For example, one instructor writes,

View full-size images from this article using this QR code or online here: http://bit.ly/1U6t816

> I think you have a strong thesis here, but I'm not sure the second half of the sentence contributes much to your argument. You might want to think about incorporating that part of your thesis earlier in your introduction. Also, while your introduction does what it needs to do, I would suggest adding a more thorough discussion of audience and purpose to help situate your reader in the rhetorical context of your essay.

In addition to its generality, as a comment on a preliminary draft to a first-year student, it assumes a vocabulary more suited to an advanced writer and offers confusing if not contradictory advice. There's nothing here that a student can directly connect to her own text; given the more abstract vocabulary used, this instructor herself appears to have little sense of audience. If, as Straub maintains, "during the time the student reads a set of comments, the image of the teacher that comes off the page becomes the teacher for that student and has an immediate impact on how those comments come to mean," (235) the student would lack a compelling image or inspiration to revise the text in question.

Another comment in this set demonstrates similar issues:

> Overall, I think you are headed in the right direction with this essay, as I can tell you understand the basic premise of a rhetorical analysis. However, there are a couple things you can work on as you begin to revise this paper. First, you need to add more analysis for this to be an effective rhetorical analysis, as you are 300 words short of the word limit. There are a few places, which I mention above, where you can expand upon your discussion of the rhetorical choices that Malcolm X uses. This will make for a more effective analysis and will also allow you to meet the word limit. Second, work on making your introduction and conclusion grab the reader's attention. There is also some room for you to expand upon your discussion of audi-

ence and purpose in your introduction and carry that throughout your draft. Finally, you may need to be more specific about your rhetorical choices or incorporate another one into your analysis to be able to be specific.

Like the first comment, this also provides the student with some mixed messages and vague advice for revision. Particularly problematic is the placement and emphasis on meeting a word count. It's one of the few concrete pieces of advice given—but if the student is having problems finding enough to write about, telling her to "expand upon your discussion" isn't going to point her in a useful direction.[10] The last sentence simply doesn't make sense. The student receiving this comment still doesn't have a clear direction or rationale (other than meeting word count) for revising her draft.

A third comment has more potential for success. The instructor highlights a specific problem (too much summary at the expense of analysis) and talks with the student about why the paper evolved in that direction. This instructor also gives the student some specific instruction (reread, identify, highlight) to get her started on her revisions.

> Your writing is relatively clear throughout the essay. The biggest problem I am seeing here is an abundance of summary rather than analysis throughout your body paragraphs. Part of the problem is your stated purpose, which sets up a summary of the text rather than an analysis of the rhetorical choices (see below). Once you are working with a purpose that focuses on "A Homemade Education" rather than the historical figure of Malcolm X, you'll want to rework your rhetorical choices and evidence so that you are analyzing specific choices made in the text rather than the author's biography. In other words, you want to focus on "how" and "why" X writes the essay, rather than simply relating "what" is being said. You mention allusion, word choice, and personal experience/anecdote in the essay. I would suggest that you reread the text and highlight as many examples of literary allusion and a specific type (formal/informal/violent/humorous/etc.) of word choice throughout the text. You can then have a better idea of how these choices are being used and connect them to your revised purpose.

From reading these and the other 100+ comments that incorporate the term *rhetorical*, as well as examining the drafts to which these comments responded to determine their contexts, I'm able to rough out a plan for our next workshop in which instructors will consider the issues revealed in these comments. The workshop following this mining session incorporated a generous sample of these instructors' comments. I mined a sample of comments from assignments that had scored between a 55 and an 88 and also pulled the drafts themselves from the database. Instructors began the workshop with a discussion of their own revision practices and of the types of commentary from instructors or peers they found helpful. We then turned to a few of the comments (acontextual), and I asked them to discuss what they believed the issues were with each draft that belonged to the comments. We then turned to the drafts, discussed those and the comments in context, and then instructors crowdsourced revised comments for those drafts. Post-workshop, I asked instructors to email me when they'd responded to 3–5 of the next revision assignment for students; after doing so, I accessed their commentary and gave them brief feedback.

Readers can see a final tenet of agile applied here—reflect at regular intervals and adjust accordingly in a meaningful timeframe that benefits current instructors and students. While it's clear from the three sample comments that substantial revision was required, the comments fall short in the instructional sense. While the instructors have been trained to identify key concepts named in all iterations of the WPA Outcomes Statement, the instructors' comments aren't helping students bridge the gap from abstraction to application of those concepts. This gap also helps explain why it's not evident to students why their drafts received the score that they did. It's critical that our new instructors spend time analyzing and revising comments on these preliminary drafts while the process of grading them is still fresh in their minds. They will be working with students for the next several weeks on revision assignments leading to the final draft submission, so the work I do with them individually and as a group will be applied immediately, to both their and their students' benefit.

Understanding Classroom Instructor, Grader, and Student Interactions

Another way in which I can study instructor behaviors and gain more insight into how both the classroom instructors and the graders, known as Document Instructors (DIs), interact with students about their writing is by examining the number of times our classroom instructors change the grades assigned to their students by the graders in their workgroups. As instructors of record, classroom instructors have the final authority to change a grade—and their frequency or reasons for doing so can point to issues I need to address in instructor training or curricular concerns. As the term progresses, trends in how many grades are amended by instructors can signal several potential points for discussion. First, if a classroom instructor is changing a significant number of her students' grades across multiple assignments and cites reasons such as "Student Grade Appeal" or "Raising a DI Grade," I need to find out why. One of the first things to look at is whether a particular grader is having her grades changed by one classroom instructor—which could signal a conflict in the interpretation of an assignment—or whether multiple graders are involved—which could suggest that the classroom instructor has a different understanding of an assignment than her graders. I would also examine the range of assignments listed—are grades being changed on a particular assignment, or are they being changed for all assignments submitted? The answers to these questions would determine whether I needed to work with the classroom instructor, with one grader, or with the entire grading workgroup to rectify the situation. If I see a widespread trend across groups, I would also look at how an assignment is written and presented to students and instructors. Regardless of cause, conversations can occur within days or weeks, resolving the problem so that both our students and instructors gain the knowledge about writing that they need. Via the use of data and agile strategies, programs have the potential to leverage their technology and data to connect more quickly with all stakeholders.

Limitations and Opportunities

The above describes several iterations of a single exploratory text mining initiative. Given the recursive and complex nature of factors influencing student and instructor activity on a single assignment, the drilling down that can take place could move in any number of directions: to examine other grades/grade ranges, to examine other components of student performance—attendance, class participation, grades, or commentary on prior scaffolded assignments. The work of instructors could also be examined through different lenses—perhaps searching for particular terms related to rhetorical knowledge, critical thinking, processes, and conventions that are included in all iterations of the WPA Outcomes Statement to determine which of these concepts are in fact being effectively communicated to students and which require a different type of commentary than new instructors are currently providing.

These tools help us develop a "culture of using data for making instructional decisions" (Bienkowski, Feng, and Means 46) throughout our program as administrators work closely with instructors to understand and assess instruction as well as address issues that surface each year as we continue to train each group of new instructors. In this more flexible environment, I analyze information that is scalable from the individual instructor to the program as a whole and have available for comparison similar information from past semesters. Having this data at my fingertips enables me, in consultation with my associate director and instructors, to make midcourse corrections literally mid-course. In doing so, we are mindful that we use this data responsibly. For example, in the above discussion concerning the changing of grades, following up with the involved instructors is paramount, especially with the instructor making the frequent changes. Understanding the motivation for such decisions is as critical for future training as the decisions themselves.

The data also provides valuable insights into the process of writing instruction at the programmatic level, information that can then be incorporated into instructor training. I can learn much about such behaviors as how instructors respond to students in their comments, what they will tend to prioritize in discussions and how they interpret a rubric. By examining instructor comments, I can also learn which assignments seem most difficult for our instructors to understand and teach. Big data contributes to this knowledge in the following way: While I might anecdotally hear a few instructors individually discuss their particular issues or understanding of an assignment, or read a few sentences about their experiences in a piece of reflective writing, that information is self reported. In looking at data—the actual commentary on hundreds of students' assignments—I can see what instructors are actually telling students about their drafts, whether they are able to provide a balance of formative and summative comments to students as appropriate, and whether any beneficial or problematic trends are endemic across the entire cohort or isolated in a few members.

For example, for several years, I found that a significant number of our instructors experienced trouble with both our literature review and rhetorical analysis assignments; consistently, those instructors' comments on preliminary drafts of these assignments fell short in some way: not showing a full understanding of how to discuss a literature review, providing the students incorrect advice, or pointing out problems in the text without providing instruction to helps students improve their drafts. In response, my associate director and I have revised our custom text, swapping out chapters deemed less effective by both instructors and students and adding custom-written material that speaks to the needs of our user groups. We've also provided far more literature review samples for instructors to use in the classroom and spent more time discussing this assignment in workshops. More recently, we've added additional requirements to our training; prior to teaching or grading a course for the first time, new instructors must write one of the major assignments for that course, along with a reflection on the process of doing so. Those assignments become part of the workshop series for the next semester. This process of doing, reflecting, and retooling is a key component of agile—especially because it takes place in a timeframe that can actually help the instructor during a semester—not six months or a year later, when they've moved on to other teaching assignments or have graduated.

Conclusion

Because it is our responsibility as administrators to create an optimal experience for our students and instructors during their time in the first-year writing program, agile research and assessment is a critical component of our program. With over 2,600 students each semester and 30 to 40 new instructors each year, I now have a way to quickly identify problems and work toward solutions that benefit both those instructors and students as well as those who follow. I can respond to Langbehn, McIntyre, and Moxley's call for real-time response and have the ability to follow and reflect on the effects of our actions as Rose recommends. While data-driven learning and assessment is predicted to impact higher education even more noticeably in the next three to five years, it will only do so if WPAs can incorporate use of the data in ways that benefit the primary stakeholders, students and instructors, as they grapple with the difficult tasks of improving their writing skills—not simply examine the data post-mortem to see what could have gone better. This type of work breaks down the boundary that some see between administrative duties and research and blends those components of a WPA's position in inextricable ways. While Bloom and others see Strickland's book as dangerous, the current emphasis on practices that improve student retention and success makes WPAs' blend of administrative and research-based tasks all the more critical. Far from being mere administrators, using big data and agile to conduct meaningful research to engage in thoughtful, yet rapid, decision making enables WPAs to rightfully claim both the research and managerial aspects of their work.

Notes

1. *Agile* in this context is a term initially applied to software development, and later to project management more generally, that encourages short, iterative cycles of planning, development, and critique. It enables users to identify problems and pose solutions more quickly than traditional, linear development paradigms.

2. Most datasets considered big data are those defined by the 3-Vs—volume, velocity, and variety—all of which are constantly growing and correspondingly more difficult to analyze and interpret as they do so. For a writing program, we might think of the 3-Vs as follows:

Volume = the number of assignments submitted

Velocity = the pace at which these assignments are submitted by students and commented upon by instructors

Variety = the type of assignments submitted, and the range of commentary given by instructors.

3. While I'm well aware of the body of substantial scholarship surrounding labor practices in higher education and in first-year writing programs, engaging that debate is beyond the scope of this article. Instead, this text focuses on the situation that we face currently. It makes the assumption that more aggressive and transparent management of a program is a positive situation—in an attempt to further the development of graduate students as instructors and improve the instruction of our first-year students.

4. The "twelve principles behind the [original] manifesto," particularly as adapted by Matthias Marschall, speak to the embedded, iterative nature of such processes as our instructor training and various levels of assessment facilitated in part by our programware.

- Our highest priority is to satisfy the customer through early and continuous delivery of valuable software.
- Welcome changing requirements, *even after deployment*, agile processes harness change for the customer's competitive advantage.
- *Upgrade* working *systems* frequently, from a couple of weeks to a couple of months, with a preference to the shorter timescale.
- Business people and *all technical staff* must work together daily throughout the *lifetime of the platform*.
- Build *platforms* around motivated individuals. Give them the environment and support they need, and trust them to get the job done.
- The most efficient and effective method of conveying information to and within a *technical* team is face-to-face conversation.
- *A working platform* is the primary measure of *success*.
- Agile processes promote sustainable *work environments*. The sponsors, *technical staff*, and users should be able to maintain a constant pace indefinitely.
- Continuous attention to technical excellence and good design enhances agility.
- Simplicity—the art of maximizing the amount of work not done—is essential.
- The best architectures, requirements, and designs emerge from self-organizing teams.
- At regular intervals, the team reflects on how to become more effective, then tunes and adjusts its behavior accordingly.

5. They suggest that those involved in instructional design and assessment ask themselves the following questions. Even a single answer of yes indicates a potential need for incorporating agile elements into the instructional and assessment processes.

- Does your team find it difficult to identify the business requirements for the learning you are designing?
- Do you find that your business requirements change frequently?
- Do your stakeholders seem resistant to adopting your recommendations?
- Does your team have access to learners so that you can observe their learning process?
- Do your requirements include adding social or informal learning to your formal learning designs?
- Do your requirements include learning measurement dashboards?
- Are your delivery schedules becoming more and more compressed?
- Do you predict that your content shelf life will be short?

6. Especially when even such fundamental documents as the WPA Outcomes Statement 3.0 are directed at those who have

> expert understanding of how students actually learn to write. For this reason, we expect the primary audience for this document to be well-prepared college writing teachers and college writing program administrators. In some places, we have chosen to write in their professional language. Among such readers, terms such as *rhetorical* and *genre* convey a rich meaning that is not easily simplified. While we have also aimed at writing a document that the general public can understand, in limited cases we have aimed first at communicating effectively with expert writing teachers and writing program administrators. (60–61)

The issue here is that for new instructors who don't have a solid foundation in teaching college writing, basic terms such as *audience* and *purpose* may not resonate enough to enable these instructors to actually help students improve their writing.

7. The software shares features of the much-maligned applications used for automated essay evaluation; however, the goal here is to bring information to the attention of WPAs and instructors to examine behaviors—not provide a final evaluation. But what should be noted is the ability of the software to provide an alternative view of textual data.

8. Both instructors and administrators also have access to each instructor's portfolio of graded work—all assignments, all instructor commentary, and, if a collaboratively graded assignment, the comments and grades given by other instructors on that assignment.

9. These assignments are presented to all group instructors with only the course and section number identified, not the name of the student. The classroom instructor, of course, has access to the full identifying information for the student in her records.

10. The comments referred to as the mentioned above comments consisted of four phrases, each of which encouraged the student to expand her discussion of a

particular rhetorical choice without providing any discussion of how the student might do so.

Works Cited

Allen, Jo. "The Impact of Student Learning Outcomes Assessment on Technical and Professional Communication Programs." *TCQ* 13.1 (2004): 93–108. Print.

Ashe, Diana. "Fostering Cultures of Great Teaching." *WPA: Writing Program Administration* 34.1 (2010): 155–61. Print.

Batt, Thomas A. "The Rhetoric of the End Comment." *Rhetoric Review* 24.2 (2005): 207–23. Print.

Beck, Kent. "Agile Manifesto." 2001. Web. 18 May 2013.

Bienkowski, Marie, Mingyu Feng, and Barbara Means. "Enhancing Teaching and Learning Through Educational Data Mining and Learning Analytics: An Issue Brief." *US Department of Education, Office of Educational Technology* (2012): 1–57. Print.

Bloom, Lynn Z. "Review of *The Managerial Unconscious in the History of Composition Studies*." *Rhetoric Review* 31.3 (2012): 350–52. Print.

Bradley, W. James. "Horizontal Assessment." *Assessment Update* 21.3 (2009): 10–11. Print.

Estrem, Heidi and E. Shelley Reid. "Writing Pedagogy Education: Instructor Development in Composition Studies." *Exploring Composition Studies: Sites, Issues, and Perspectives*. Ed. Kelly Ritter and Paul Kei Matsuda. Boulder: UP of Colorado, 2012. 223–40. Print.

Groves, Amy, Catherine Rickelman, Connie Cassarino, and M J Hall. "Are You Ready for Agile Learning Design?" *T+D* (2012): 46–51. Print.

Johnson, Larry, Samantha Adams Becker, Victoria Estrada, and Alex Freeman. *NMC Horizon Report: 2014 Higher Education Edition*. Austin, Texas: The New Media Consortium, 2014. Print.

Kemp, Fred. "Computers, Innovation, and Resistance in First-Year Composition." *Discord and Direction: The Postmodern Writing Program Administrator*. Ed. Sharon J. McGee and Carolyn Handa. Logan: Utah State P, 2005. 105–22. Print.

Langbehn, Karen, Megan McIntyre, and Joseph Moxley. "Re-Mediating Writing Program Assessment." *Digital Writing Assessment & Evaluation*. Ed. Heidi A McKee and Dànielle N. DeVoss. Logan: Utah State UP, 2013. *Computers and Composition Digital Press*. Web. 8 Apr. 2013.

Marschall, Matthias. "The 12 principles Behind the Agile Manifesto Adapted to Web Operations." *Agile Web Development and Operations* 7 Aug. 2009. Web. 25 Apr. 2013.

McKee, Heidi. A., and Dànielle N. DeVoss, eds. *Digital Writing Assessment & Evaluation*. Logan: Utah State University P, 2013. *Computers and Composition Digital Press*. Web. 8 Apr. 2013.

Moxley, Joseph M. "Big Data, Learning Analytics, and Social Assessment Methods." *Journal of Writing Assessment* 6.1 (2013). Web. 15 Aug. 2013.

Reid, E. Shelley, Heidi Estrem, and Marcia Belcheir. "The Effects of Writing Pedagogy Education on Graduate Teaching Assistants' Approaches to Teaching Composition." *WPA: Writing Program Administration* 36.1 (2012): 32–73. Print.

Rose, Shirley K. "The WPA Within: WPA Identities and Implications for Graduate Education in Rhetoric and Composition." *College English* 75.2 (2012): 218–30.

Schwieger, Dana, and Ken Surendran. "Information Technology Management: Course Re-design Using an Assessment Driven Approach." *2012 Proceedings of the Information Systems Educators Conference* 29.1922 (2012): 1–14. Print.

Smith, Summer. "The Genre of the End Comment: Conventions in Teacher Responses to Student Writing." *College Composition and Communication* 48.2 (1997): 249–68. Print.

Sommers, Nancy. "Responding to Student Writing." *College Composition and Communication* 33.2 (1982): 148–56. Print.

Straub, Richard. "The Concept of Control in Teacher Response: Defining the Varieties of 'Directive' and 'Facilitative' Commentary." *College Composition and Communication* 47.2 (1996): 223–51. Print.

Strickland, Donna. *The Managerial Unconscious in the History of Composition Studies*. Carbondale: Southern Illinois UP, 2011. Print.

Taggart, Amy Rupiper, and Margaret Lowry. "Cohorts, Grading, and *Ethos*: Listening to TAs Enhances Teacher Preparation." *WPA: Writing Program Administration* 34.2 (2011): 89–114. Print.

Wasley, Paula. "A New Way to Grade." *The Chronicle of Higher Education* 10 Mar. 2006: A6-A8. Print.

Susan M. Lang is Professor and Director of the First-Year Writing Program in the Technical Communication and Rhetoric Division of the Department of English at Texas Tech University, a public Carnegie Tier 1 university. She teaches courses in data and text mining, writing program administration, social media integration, other aspects of technical communication, and rhetoric and composition. She has published in College English, College Composition and Communication, Computers and Composition, JTWC, *and various edited collections.*

An Institutional Ethnography of Information Literacy Instruction: Key Terms, Local/Material Contexts, and Instructional Practice

Michelle LaFrance

ABSTRACT

This essay shares the results of a three-year study on the circulation of information literacy *as a key term in a First-Year Writing (FYW) program at a mid-sized branch campus. Tracing the use of the term* information literacy *as it shape-shifted through sites of instruction, teaching conversations, and other moments in the program was revealing of the material conditions, ruling relations, and standpoints active in the program's classrooms. Findings revealed that instructors negotiated the term as an enactment of quite personal value systems, demonstrating highly individual understandings of the role of FYW in the preparation of student writers as researchers. Instructors and library faculty enacted teaching practices around the term differently in order to manage the material conditions that influenced their everyday relations in classrooms, the library, and across campus. The realization that FYW instructors and library faculty employed the term towards very different ends was a generative moment, providing a data-driven understanding of how our ongoing collaborative conversations might be framed differently.*

As Eileen Schell writes, "One of the most important aspects of research methods and methodologies in rhetoric, composition, and literacy scholarship has been the concerted effort to analyze and assess how writing, rhetoric, and literacy practices have been shaped by material constraints and realities" (123). Teaching practices do not take shape in isolation from their material surroundings. They are the mindful actions of people who are influenced by and invested in local materialities, such as the social relations, available resources, and prevailing value systems within and across campus communities. Understanding the interconnections between material realities and teaching practices is particularly important for WPAs, who are frequently called upon to explain how things are happening in classrooms, placement processes, assessment activities, and the many other procedures and pedagogies that organize faculty and student work within writing programs.

This essay explores information literacy instruction at a mid-sized branch campus (MSBC) using the methodological framework of institutional ethnography (IE), a methodology attuned to the material concerns of writing program work. The result of a three-year study of the way the key term *information literacy* shape-shifted in the teaching conversations of a first-year writing program, the data gathered through this project demonstrates what we've long suspected and discussed as WPAs: a yawning gap often exists between what actually happens within a program or a classroom and the professional statements, disciplinary conversations, or ongoing research-based understandings of best practice in the field at large. In the end, on the MSBC campus, the material conditions of the campus community and the local sensibilities of faculty drove the use of the term in FYW courses.

When I arrived at MSBC—a school of 8,000 undergraduates that typically offered around 65 sections of FYW each semester (staffed almost entirely with adjunct labor)—information literacy was already an active term in many of the teaching conversations central to work in FYW. I was puzzled that this term was such a central force in FYW, as the term was not a feature of the outcomes for the FYW courses (a two-course 100-level sequence), which referenced research activities for student writers, calling upon students to "Incorporate and accurately document outside sources using proper documentation format" and to "Select, effectively integrate, and document appropriate resource materials from library databases and print holdings," respectively. Even so, the term information literacy recurred in conversations with instructors, faculty, and administrators (even in the absence of library representatives) and seemed to hold deep, but different, significance for many individuals across the institution. This study brought to light the divergent array of teaching practices umbrella-ed under the term in the FYW program and helped me, as WPA, understand that FYW instructors most often discussed and enacted the term in response to the local/material conditions that informed their individual sense of the program's mission. As the study progressed, I gained important understandings of the complex program I directed and how it responded to the exigencies of our unique institutional contexts.

Louise Phelps once noted that writing programs can have a well-articulated central vision but may still be sites of "tensions and oscillations between order and chaos" (172) and demonstrate "huge disparities and variations among [teaching] experiments" (173). Likewise, the presence of a key term in program conversations can be deceptive. This study demonstrates that a term such as information literacy may act as a generalizing force, lending an illusory sense of pedagogical connection to national and professional discussions of writing pedagogy, when in fact the teaching practices that it encompasses may be influenced far more dramatically by local constraints, values, and relationships to others on campus. As this study traced how the term shape-shifted in different sites of instruction and a variety of conversations about teaching research, it became clear that national and professional discourses, such as the Association of College and Research Libraries' (ACRL) Information Literacy Standards, the WPA Outcomes Statement, or other current understandings of composition pedagogy (such as teaching for transfer or the rhetorical situation) held less sway over what actually happened in classrooms or library sessions than did an array of highly local, materially-inflected relationships, beliefs, and constraints.

Exploration of a Key Term: The IE Framework and Methods

In this study, I approached the key term *information literacy* as a dynamic problematic or "situated point of entry" (LaFrance and Nicolas 151) into the complex processes of decision-making, spheres of influence, and routine that were the writing program in action. I have written elsewhere with Melissa Nicolas about institutional ethnography (IE), noting that IE asks researchers to uncover the empirical connections between individual practice and the conditions that make a site of study unique. Work with IE reveals how "organizational context invisibly shapes the [professional] practices of a site" (Townsend 179). To that end, I was interested in analyzing how teaching practices in the writing program were mediated by the material realities and social relations of our campus, particularly the constraints of contingent employment status and the impact of our collaboration with the under-resourced campus library.

Qualitative data-collection activities for this project spanned three years and included the survey of adjunct instructors in the program (23 of then 28); observations and notes from collaborative work within the program and with the libraries; a review of relevant documents (assignments, handouts, library resources, and readings); and a series of focus groups (four total groups with three to five participants in each) and one-on-one interviews (fifteen total) with FYW instructors and faculty in the disciplines. In surveys, interviews, and focus groups, first-year writing instructors were asked to share basic identifying information (including educational background), their definitions of the term, whether they invited library staff to work with their classes, as well as any instructional concerns, teaching strategies, and challenges faced when teaching information literacy-related skills. Subsequent interviews and focus groups asked participants to look over summarized results from survey data and comment upon the initial findings, expanding upon their own original answers and the trends represented.

The constraints upon this study are important to note: Because this project began with a concern for how the term circulated exclusively in the FYW program, librarians and a large sample of faculty outside of English were not recruited to participate in the survey, interview, or focus groups. Instead, online source texts produced by library staff and ongoing, public discussions about the FYW/library collaboration provide the primary (textual and observational) data for this study—field-oriented sources of data that have long been valued within the ethnographic tradition.

All responses, observation notes, and textual data were analyzed for emergent patterns (typically, frequency of response), following the grounded theory model (Glaser; Strauss and Corbin). Two heuristics central to the secondary analysis of data were "ruling relations" and standpoint (Smith *Sociology*). Smith describes ruling relations as "that extraordinary yet ordinary complex of relations . . . that connect us across space and time and organize our everyday lives" (Practice 8). Standpoint theory holds that "knowledge is always socially situated" (Harding 7). In the juxtaposition of these terms, IE asks researchers to think about how participants co-construct institutional sites through their daily work. Differences of practice and meaning are always a given in the IE framework; as such, I particularly sought to understand how unique definitions of the term circulated through the many ways of doing, knowing, and being that constituted our program. To ensure the reliability of this study, I triangulated the findings across data collected via participant observation, online survey, interview, focus group, and analysis of documents. As categories of response emerged, initial findings were reassessed and re-developed to attend to the complexities across data sets.

Ruling Relations: National Disciplinary and Professional Tensions

For disciplinary professionals such as WPAs, ruling relations are established norms of professional discourse, organized by the national organizations, statements, standards, noteworthy publications, and subsequent best practices central to the work of particular communities or professional fields. The WPA Outcomes Statement or the ACRL Information Literacy Standards, for instance, offer educators a sense of the ideals of practice and prevailing sensibilities within their disciplines. As epistemological frameworks, these statements idealize aspects of student learning, endorsing and sanctioning particular types of practice and very specific understandings of work with students and colleagues.

The ACRL established the definition of *information literacy* in 1989 when the organization first indexed the term as a "set of abilities" requiring individuals to "recognize when information is needed and have the ability to locate, evaluate, and use effectively the needed information" (n. pag.). As they have redeveloped the term over time—for instance, publishing a lengthy list of competencies for information literacy instruction in 2001 and establishing a new framework for understanding how information is created, granted value, and then circulated in 2015—the ACRL has tried to account for the rapidly changing landscape of education, especially as technology has altered the nature of library services and ideals of research practice at large. Twenty-five years after the ACRL's original definition was released, librarians, libraries, and library journals continue to lead in the circulation of the term, often inadvertently reinforcing the campus library as the primary hub for all research activity on campuses.

I will note here that this study took place before the ACRL's revisions to the Information Literacy Standards were made public in 2015 (see Malenfant-IL). With the revision of the information literacy competencies into the new Framework for Information Literacy, collaborations between libraries and writing program has continued, as leaders in the conversation hope to create clearer connections between the ACRL's understandings of information literacy and the ways FYW classes and other writing programs teach research. The ACRL has hosted a series of online workshops about first-year writing program and library collaborations, for instance ["Innovative"]), building upon previous efforts to overcome the difficulties that arise when separate disciplinary communities collaborate (see Maid and D'Angelo or Brady et al.).

Complicating this discussion, the field of Writing Studies has dozens of different critical conversations about what research is and what sorts of instruction students as researchers need, a series of ruling contests that shape pedagogical approaches in quite different ways. From Manning's query in 1961 about whether the research paper was here to stay, to Macrorie's *I-Search* essay that pitched research as a form of inquiry, to Bizup's call to teach research as a rhetorical practice, to Wardle's critique of Composition's reliance on mutt genres including the research paper, to efforts by the Citation Project team to understand source usage (see Jamieson and Howard), there is ample discussion of research even if there is little agreement in the field of Writing Studies about what constitutes research or how students best learn the basic conventions of research. In fact, some recent research efforts around writing transfer put enormous pressure on many of the traditional efforts to teach research in composition classrooms at all (see Downs and Wardle 2007).

A number of sources published in library science venues have treated the resulting structural difficulties of collaboration between libraries and writing programs. D'Angelo and Maid note the frustrations and barriers that complicate library and composition collaborations when faculty in the disciplines oversee curricular developments and librarians are positioned as consultants. These relationships are further complicated by the low prestige granted library faculty—a situation that mirrors the low status or prestige granted contingent faculty who teach writing courses. Likewise, McGuinness and Saunders acknowledge that the campus library conversations about information literacy standards often exclude input from faculty across the curriculum. Mazziotta and Gretano are very clear about the persistence required to find connections between the former ACRL Information Literacy Standards and the WPA Outcomes Statements. These scholarly projects reveal that the concerns, interests, and notions of best practice central to professional conversations about writing program pedagogy and administration may simply be foreign to campus librarians and difficult to implement for contingent faculty.

Standpoint and the Local

Standpoint recognizes the dynamism of individuals as they negotiate the discursive patterns and highly localized realities of writing programs—an awareness particularly important for WPAs, who must rhetorically negotiate the many different investments on a campus. Individuals are always situated within the material, engaging in highly personal association(s) with institutional histories, memories, and patterns. As such, an individual's social alliances, experiences, and sensibilities play a defining role in how that individual negotiates everyday institutional settings such as classrooms, programs, or departments.

Recent research in Writing Studies has shown that local relationships exert enormous force on the pedagogical investments of instructors in FYW programs. Estrem and Reid have shown, for instance, that the primary pedagogical influences for TAs as new teachers are the local peers/other TAs with whom they work most closely in graduate programs. Grettano, Ingalls, and Morse write eloquently about the resistance of faculty they worked with to the WPA Outcomes Statement—entrenched local values were simply at odds with the value systems embraced by the Outcomes Statement. Just as tellingly, Brannon and Scott illuminated crucial differences exhibited in approaches to writing assessment between tenure-line faculty and instructors in the same program: tenure-line faculty "established their expertise with their peers through staking out different positions in writing education," while non-tenure-line instructors tended to focus on "the teaching they have done for years in this program," and a consensus-based sense of what mattered most in student writing. Surface concerns ultimately mattered most in non-tenure-line conversations—while tenure-line faculty favored rhetorical moves, questions of style, or notions of audience (284). These studies demonstrate the importance for ethnographers who work in institutional locations to account for standpoint. Our thinking about writing and writing instruction may not only be foreign to those we work with across campus; the ideas WPAs embrace may indeed be foreign to people working within the programs we lead.

MSBC's local and material factors persistently shaped conversations about the relationship between information literacy and student writing instruction. MSBC had struggled financially for over a decade due to the consistent decline in state funding. The material conditions of campus were particularly dire: Classrooms and buildings were in disrepair. As enrollments had grown, classroom space had not. It was difficult for writing classes to book into the nearly obsolete computer classrooms (which had persistent issues connecting to online resources such as the library web site). Instructors often negotiated the limitations of classrooms and digital tools in very creative ways—using static screen captures of the library's web pages in lieu of real-time online access or putting together extensive step-by-step handouts that described the processes of research. Cutbacks to the library budget had required that many senior library faculty, including those who had previously only worked with upper division students, staff information desks and provide instructional support for FYW courses.

Faculty at all ranks (in and outside of the FYW program) frequently expressed dismay that first-year students were not prepared for college-level writing. These conversations often posed instructors affiliated with the FYW as gatekeepers and interrogators of student work—a role at times embraced by a number of instructors who believed that correctness was the central feature of effective writing. Conversations about student deficiencies, corresponding with a desire that writing instruction focus on policing student texts, often dampened initiatives to support student writers in other ways. In a meeting with me about FYW and library collaboration, for example, senior library faculty quite vocally asserted that it was the FYW program's job, first and foremost, to teach students "how to write sentences." These same library faculty steadfastly asserted that first-year students were prepared only for the most basic of search tools available through the library's web site—tools that tended to access popular sources, such as newspapers and magazines, over scholarly journals, trade journals, or other venues for research intended for professional and disciplinary audiences. At the same time, the English library liaison also insistently voiced the desire that "one-shot" sessions become a requirement for all FYW classes. These 50-minute sessions brought FYW classes into one of the library's computer labs. The library faculty who led them typically provided a series of search terms based upon the current assignment in the class, highlighted one or two search tools on the library's web site, and demonstrated the process of finding sources via one or two of those search tools. As the English library liaison confided to me in one of several meetings about our collaborations, these sessions were essential because "We need to keep students from going to the reference desk."

In light of these conversations, it often appeared that the library staff saw their work with the FYW program as a means to prescribe how students should conduct research and access the library and its overwhelmed services. These material conditions dramatically shaped our collaborations, reducing the library's role to discussions about finding the correct sorts of sources over other aspects of information literacy as defined by the ACRL at the time. While the library faculty and instructors involved in the FYW program all valued helping students become more sophisticated users of research tools, we simply did not share a vision for how instruction around research tools might be carried out or teaching a more expansive understanding of information literacy.

Tracing *Information Literacy*: Disciplinary, Professional, and Personal Relationships

> *Historically at the center of the university's intellectual process, the [MSBC] Library is many things to many people. It is the librarian working with a student in the discovery and evaluation of search methods and knowledge resources. It is the physical building with its collections, it is seating for group study and individual contemplation. It is a virtual space with resources that are accessible at anytime from anywhere.*
>
> —MSBC Library Vision, Values, and Commitment Statement

Three years of IE data gathering—the careful unearthing of ruling relations and exploration of standpoints—were required to map the complicated interrelationships proliferating through information literacy instruction in the program. The examples in this section show individuals personally negotiating the different ideals of the term in relation to their own investments, professional positions, relationships, and pedagogical leanings within the local landscape. In pointing out the disjunctions I uncovered, my intent is less to identify (good or bad) camps than to reveal how personal differences and local constraints made a significant difference in typical uses of the term and the work it came to actualize.

Overall data reveals that use of the term corresponded with demonstrations of anxiety around the growth of unsanctioned search tools, sources, and research practices. The library—often cited by survey respondents (17 of 23) as the source of the term's popularity on campus—deployed discussions about information literacy in ways that endorsed a prescriptive use of library resources. FYW instructors' responses are less cohesive in this sense but demonstrate unevenness in understanding and application of the term, while also foregrounding the primacy of the library in efforts to discuss, describe, and organize research undertakings. The majority of FYW and library faculty seemed to center on correctness over broader understandings of research, such as how to understand when library-based research was necessary, the sort of evidence needed to persuasively argue a position, evaluate evidence once found, or other elements of academic literacy central to professional statements such as the ACRL standards and the WPA Outcomes.

The "ENL 101 Lib Guide"

The MSBC library website provides resources for student researchers, including lists of area-specific search engines, web pages that offer information or explain key resources, tips and research strategies, and resources for navigating the particularities of the library. The "ENL 101 Lib Guide" supported the library's one-shot sessions for FYW classes (see fig 1), offering a general orientation to the library web page, information on finding books and journal articles, and citation style guides. At the time of this study (the guide has since been removed from the library's web site), the guide included a tab on "Information Literacy," which offered a side bar titled "What is Information Literacy?" The page provided a link to the ACRL website and this definition: "Information Literacy is the set of skills needed to find, retrieve, analyze, and use information." Readers familiar with the ACRL's 2004 definition of *information literacy*—one of the national ruling relations identified in this study—may recognize the descriptions of the sub-skills listed on this tab, as the guide borrows ACRL's language verbatim and without citation.

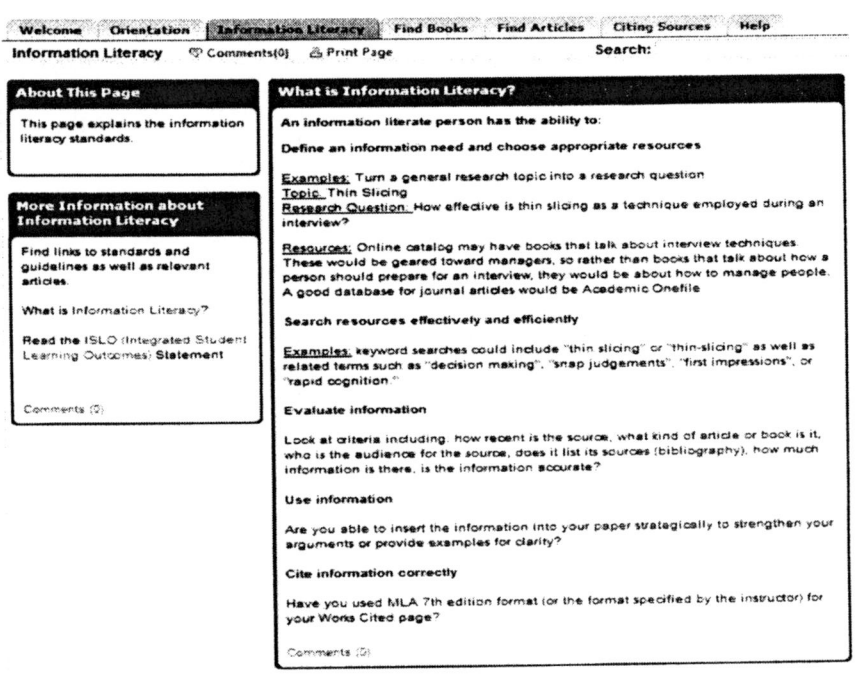

Fig. 1. MSBC library ENL. 101 library guide

Each header references one of the skill sets central to ACRL's definition at the time of the study. A few words are also offered to provide further context, offer specific practices, or highlight resources: "An Information Literate person is able to: Recognize and define the need for information . . . Define an information need and choose appropriate resources . . . Search resources effectively and efficiently . . . Evaluate information . . . Use information . . . [and] Cite information correctly." The broad abilities identified by the ACRL are broken into smaller tasks such as "choosing and narrowing a topic," "identifying search terms," "asking a series of questions about the sources located," and "strategically strengthening your arguments." Readers are directed to "key word searches," local resources such as the "online catalog," "books and articles," and the "MLA 7th edition format." The paragraph under "Resources," reads: "Online catalog may have books that talk about interview techniques. A good database for journal articles would be Academic OneFile." The paragraph about "Examples" reads: "keyword search could include 'thin slicing' or 'thin-slicing,' as well as related terms such as 'decision making,' 'snap judgments,' 'first impressions,' or 'rapid cognition.'"

Discussion

The "Lib Guide" demonstrates a number of tensions circulating between the ruling definitions of *information literacy* as a key term in a disciplinary or professional sense and how the term deployed locally to reflect value systems around correctness at work at MSBC. Because the site was designed to be the background for one-shot library sessions with a librarian, there is little explanation of the terms or processes. Even as the guide nods to the broad literacies central to the definition posed by the ACRL, it slips into prescribing student practice via a step-by-step process for researchers to follow. Over all, the focus remains on a rote process of finding sources via the library, with little attention given to the broader aspects of the term.

In referencing the ACRL, the guide draws on the professional organization as a source of legitimation for particular types of research practice, centering the campus library as the key source for the information literate individual. This focus situates library faculty as the stewards of research and reinforces the library itself as the site that sanctions effective research. While the guide does make direct reference to a portion of the FYW curriculum ("thin slicing" from *Blink,* the summer reading), it reduces "sources" to "books and articles" and reifies the MLA sourcebook as the primary source for citation practice. These moves reinforce notions of correctness as central to the research activities of FYW students.

FYW Instructor Definitions, Discussions of Practice

Another set of tensions became clearer as I began to analyze how instructors described *information literacy*. The survey and interview scripts asked participants to describe their most recent educational experiences, whether they scheduled one-shot sessions with the library faculty in their FYW courses, how well library collaborations worked in their courses, and to describe their challenges and teaching strategies as instructors. These questions allowed me to triangulate participant's affinities across different types of responses.

FYW instructors who indicated in survey, interview, and focus group responses that they worked closely with the library staff (17 of 23) tended to foreground a series of rules about conducting research and rote approaches to student research practice. These instructors often discussed information literacy in light of how their students failed to meet their expectations. For example, an instructor who responded very positively to the question "How would you characterize the library's support services for your work with students around information literacy?" also noted in a later response about the challenges of information literacy instruction: "The library is helpful—Wikipedia not so much!"

On the other hand, FYW instructors who did not indicate a close working relationship with the library faculty tended to indicate that they held broader ideas about research activities. These individuals often indicated on survey and interview responses that they had recent experiences in graduate school or continuing education practicums (6 of 23). They tended to discuss information literacy in relation to an array of possible practices and literacies, including research methods not associated with the library: ethnographic observation, cultural critique, strategic reading, and/or exploration of the strengths and limitations of tools such as Google. Their concern was for the effective support of student research as a form of critical inquiry and problem solving, over particular uses of the library and preferred tools.

Overall, survey, interview, and focus group findings revealed that the majority of FYW instructors (17 of 23) conceived of information literacy as a fixed, arhetorical need to find sources. These same instructors indicated that they privileged library-based research practices, particularly use of the library's search tools to find scholarly or peer-reviewed sources for use in student writing. But, most significantly, this tendency to reduce the term to searching for certain types of pre-approved sources was overwhelmingly true for those individuals who identified that they learned about the term from the campus library (13 of 23). We can see an immediate echo between the "Lib Guide" definition above and the following interview response, for instance:

> Participant 6: Usually when I break it down for students, I say 'It's steps.' Being able to understand the directions, what you're being asked to look for. Being able to find the resources that you need to find that information. Being able to gather that information. Being able to process that information. So it's a step-by-step process.

This indicated to me the degree to which many FYW faculty embraced prescriptive understandings of research practice in their writing classes, an approach shared and encouraged by library faculty, as I have discussed above.

Interestingly, several FYW instructors from this same grouping (13 of 23) tended to exhibit quite a bit of anxiety around the reliability of general online sources, students' information-seeking behaviors, the ability of students to evaluate texts for credibility, avoid plagiarism, and adhere to correctness in citation/documentation of sources. Members of this group of instructors noted that they spent a good amount of time teaching citation practices in their classes (10 of 23). One respondent noted, for instance, "We go over the styles extensively and yet [students] are still confused. It is frustrating for me." Another described his/her challenges in teaching information literacy simply as, "Citations, citations, citations."

Another small group of faculty (7 of 23) noted that their discussions of information literacy were most focused on dissuading plagiarism. These instructors tended to voice distaste toward commonly bemoaned student research behaviors, particularly the use of widely available online research tools. Google and/or Wikipedia were frequent targets for casual vehemence, and a number of responses persistently pitted the library's resources against Internet-based resources, noting, for instance:

> I recognize that most students will rely on Google whenever possible . . .
>
> [I]nformation literacy includes the ability to use technology and databases to find and use relevant information of high quality (not Wikipedia, Google, *National Enquirer*, bozos-r-us.com).

Moreover, members of this group of respondents also tended to characterize students as underprepared, often resistant to learning, or simply uninterested in more sanctioned forms of research. An example:

> [Students] just want to Google crap and then comment poach it in and call it good. They are not interested in learning about their topics (even when they choose them). They simply want to get the paper written as fast as possible.

References to student information seeking behaviors among this group of instructors are almost entirely negative, characterizing their students as disinterested, even lazy, researchers. "IT'S BORING and students don't connect what they do on one paper to the larger academic community," one instructor noted. Another shared that "Students do not critically evaluate the credibility of sources. They often do not ask good research-based questions despite prodding. Usually they are content to 'dump' information at me, not worrying about synthesizing or analyzing it."

In contrast, instructors who were more likely to challenge definitions of *information literacy* received from library-related sources (6 of 23) often worked to expand the range of practices available to them as teachers. Consider the following responses about information literacy instruction:

> Participant 7: I think many students feel that they are very information literate because they know how to do a Google search. So my goal is to get them beyond a simple Google search and getting them to see that there are better ways to search for information. And that includes using Google.

Participant 9: When I hear other people talk about the term, I hear them talking about going to the library and looking things up. It isn't about the process of inquiry. It isn't about the process of evaluating sources—reflecting on why we use sources.

Participant 2: Restrictions on types of sources students can use in their papers just seem to end up being counterproductive. Some sources are reliable or relevant or strong, but students have found them on their own—they haven't gone through the library's databases.

Participant 4: A lot of what will be happening in this research process is that my students will be gathering general information about their communities. And specific information about one community. . . . and that will lead me outside of the typical realm of academic research. So I guess the question that comes up for me is what is academic research? What is it not?

Discussion

The responses of faculty instructors in the FYW revealed the complexity and constraints of our local conditions. All faculty in FYW aligned their teaching practices with personal beliefs, but for many faculty, the primary belief driving their teaching of information literacy was that correctness mattered most. These beliefs often closely reproduced broader campus values for instilling correctness into student behavior and work. Others aligned their teaching practices as a reflection of personal experiences and beliefs gained from graduate studies or continuing education programs.

Understanding the quite different standpoints of FYW instructors as a reflection of the everyday material realities that instructors negotiated allowed me to also understand how FYW instructors were approaching information literacy instruction in their classes. Performing different allegiances to personal ideals in their teaching was perhaps one means by which instructors managed the unwieldy nature of teaching research—some simplified the nature of research in their classes while a smaller subset presented research endeavors as a rhetorical and problem-solving enterprise. In most cases, as this data reveals, personal beliefs (especially around correctness and sanctioning particular types of activities over others) and relationships on campus were a far more pressing concern than reflecting the broader values demonstrated by statements like the WPA Outcomes or notions of *information literacy* central to the ACRL Standards.

Conclusion: A Data-Driven Local Picture

The findings of this study are particularly timely in light of the ACRL's redefinition of *information literacy* and subsequent possibilities for renewed collaborations between writing programs and library faculty. This study lends insights into the sorts of beliefs and related practices some WPAs may encounter as they discuss the revised framework with colleagues on their campuses and in their programs. The divergences I uncovered in the course of this study enabled me to understand far more strategically where to begin conversations I hoped to foster via professional development and how to more strategically target information literacy instruction in the FYW program I then directed.

WPAs benefit from this sort of inquiry into the key terms of the programs they lead. The study of how teaching is shaped in relation to site-specific materialities, such as social relations, beliefs, and other constraints allows us to understand the many different—highly personal, always locally inflected, and materially mediated—ways the people that we work with make decisions and teach within a program. Our local conditions have extraordinary power to overwrite, refuse, ignore, or resist the professional discourses that shape the broader field. Because a key term, like *information literacy*, indexes so many different cross-institutional concerns, its use may easily become a site of local contest. Librarians and FYW faculty alike may willingly embrace a key term to demonstrate their desire to serve students and a campus community but may do so in ways that diverge from the pedagogical currents of national statements and more recent research-driven findings about effective practice. A deeper understanding and appreciation of what is happening within a program and across a campus may emerge from the process of study of these differences.

As WPA, this study enabled me to take a few informed steps toward shaping the conversation about information literacy in our program to be more reflective of ongoing national conversations:

1. I worked closely with a FYW instructor who shared my interest in offering new models for the one-shot library sessions. We developed a new session that highlighted the rhetorical and disciplinarily-inflected nature of the search for information, building on the work some FYW instructors were already doing. This session asked students to read a scholarly essay in their chosen field or major (selecting an example from a collection of essays provided by the FYW instructor). The library faculty was then asked to offer a shorter session that supported students in first critically evaluating and then finding two of the sources listed in the bibliography

of the essay they had read. Our hope with this new model was to demonstrate that different types of writing tasks would require different approaches to finding and evaluating sources.

2. I worked with this same FYW faculty member to develop a series of online, reusable learning tools that focused on practical concerns around the use of Google and Wikipedia in writing classes. (If we could not dissuade students from thinking of these tools as the go-to sites for research—or instructors from feeling anxiety about the tools—we could still have a conversation about what these tools did and did not enable us to do as researchers.) Instructors could ask students to view and reflect upon these videos inside or outside of classes.

3. I also asked the FYW instructors who had been excited by the ideas we were discussing in our interviews and focus groups to help me put together a series of workshops for their colleagues in FYW about information literacy. To complement other curricular revisions, we compiled and circulated several different models of FYW assignments that reimagined the nature of research projects.

The realization that FYW instructors and the library faculty employed the term *information literacy* to enact sometimes quite personal values and to reflect different experiences of the material realities of our campus was a generative moment for me as a WPA. Understanding more about the overlapping and competing forces at work when we used the term helped me to consider more than just problems we were facing; it required me to think through the degree to which individual teaching practices were often the responsive products of local sensibilities and undeniable materialities beyond my control. Approaching the program as a site of proliferation and difference also informed my understandings about what we valued in common, what aspects of institutional mission we might also share, and how these mutual investments informed what we actually did in our classrooms.

Work with institutional ethnography may provide WPAs in other settings with equally useful and data-driven insights into perpetually thorny administrative questions and issues. WPAs who are more attuned to the many different value systems and material realities at work within programs, who better understand how personal value systems shape classroom practice in understandable ways, are more effectively situated to support those in their programs in their everyday work, to usher in new curricular direction as necessary, and to respond to the actual conditions that subtend classroom practice.

Works Cited

Association of College and Research Libraries. "Information Literacy Competency Standards for Higher Education." *American Library Association.* 18 Jan. 2000. Web. 5 Jan. 2013.

—. "Framework for Information Literacy for Higher Education. *American Library Association.* 11 Jan. 2016. Web. 13 Jan. 2016.

Brady, Laura, Nathalie Singh-Corcoran, Jo Ann Dadisman, and Kelly Diamond. "A Collaborative Approach to Information Literacy: First-Year Composition, Writing Center, and Library Partnerships at West Virginia University." *Composition Forum* 19 (2009): n. pag. Web. 15 Dec. 2013.

Bizup, Joseph. "BEAM: A Rhetorical Vocabulary for Teaching Research-Based Writing." *Rhetoric Review* 27.1 (2008): 72–86. Print.

Brannon, Lil, and Tony Scott. "Democracy, Struggle, and the Praxis of Assessment." *College Composition and Communication* 65.2 (2013): 273–98. Print.

D'Angelo, Barbara J., and Barry M. Maid. "Moving Beyond Definitions: Implementing Information Literacy across the Curriculum." *Journal of Academic Librarianship* 30.3 (2004): 212–16. Print.

Downs, Doug, and Elizabeth Wardle. "Teaching about Writing, Righting Misconceptions: (Re)Envisioning 'First Year Composition' as 'Introduction to Writing Studies.'" *College Composition and Communication* 58.4 (2007): 552–84. Print.

Estrem, Heidi, and E. Shelley Reid. "What New Writing Teachers Talk About When They Talk About Teaching." *Pedagogy* 12.3 (2012): 447–78. Print.

Glaser, Barney G. *Basics of Grounded Theory Analysis: Emerging vs. Forcing.* Valley: Sociology Press, 1992. Print.

Grettano, Teresa, Rebecca Ingalls, and Tracy Ann Morse. "The Perilous Vision of the Outcomes Statement." *The WPA Outcomes Statement: A Decade Later.* Ed. Nicholas N. Behm, Gregory R. Glau, Deborah H. Holdstein, Duane Roen, and Edward M. White. Anderson: Parlor P, 2013. 45–57. Print.

Harding, Sandra. "Introduction: Standpoint Theory as a Site of Political, Philosophic, and Scientific Debate." *The Feminist Standpoint Theory Readers: Intellectual and Political Controversies.* Ed. Sandra Harding. Routledge: Sage, 2004. 1–15. Print.

Harrington, Susanmarie, Rita Malencyzk, Irv Peckham, Keith Rhodes, and Kathleen Blake Yancey. "WPA Outcomes Statement for First-Year Composition." Version 2.0 July 2008. Council of Writing Program Administrators. Web. 10 Aug. 2013.

Horner, Bruce. *Terms of Work for Composition: A Materialist Critique.* Albany: State U of New York P, 2000. Print.

"Innovative Instructional Partnerships for Librarians and Writing Faculty." ACRL e-Learning Webcast Series: Framing the Framework Series. American Library Association. February 10, 2016. Web. 10 Feb. 2016.

LaFrance, Michelle, and Melissa Nicolas. "Institutional Ethnography as Materialist Framework for Writing Program Research and the Faculty-Staff Work

Standpoints Project." *Research Methodology.* Spec issue of *College Composition and Communication.* 64.1 (2012): 130–50. Print.

Macrorie, Ken. *The I-Search Paper.* Portsmouth: Heinemann, 1988. Print.

Maid, Barry, and Barbara D'Angelo. "The WPA Outcomes, Information Literacy, and Challenges of Outcomes-Based Curricular Design." *Writing Assessment in the 21st Century: Essays in Honor of Edward M. White.* Ed. Norbert Elliot and Les Perelman. New York: Hampton P, 2012. 99–112. Print.

Malenfant-IL, Kara. "Information Literacy Standards Committee Feedback on Revised Draft Framework." *ALA Connect.* American Library Association, 24 June 2014. Web. 18 Oct. 2015.

Manning, Ambrose N. "The Present Status of the Research Paper in Freshman English: A National Survey." *College Composition and Communication* 12 (1961): 73–78. Print.

Mazziotta, Donna, and Teresa Grettano. "'Hanging Together': Collaboration Between Information Literacy and Writing Programs Based on the ACRL Standards and the WPA Outcomes." ACRL 2011 Conference Proceedings. 30 Mar.-4 Apr. 2011. Web. 7 July 2014.

McGuinness, Claire. "What Faculty Think—Exploring the Barriers to Information Literacy Development in Undergraduate Education." *The Journal of Academic Librarianship* 32.6 (2006): 573–82. Print.

MSBC Campus Library. "ENL 101 Lib Guide." n. d. Web. 1 Jan. 2013.

Phelps, Louise Wetherbee. "Telling the Writing Program Its Own Story: A Tenth-Anniversary Speech." *The Writing Program Administrator as Researcher: Inquiry in Action and Reflection.* Ed. Shirley K Rose and Irwin Weiser. Boynton/Cook Heinemann, 1999. 168–84. Print.

Saunders, Laura. "Faculty Perspectives on Information Literacy as a Student Learning Outcome." *The Journal of Academic Librarianship* 38.4 (2012): 226–36. Print.

Schell, Eileen. "Materializing the Material as a Progressive Method and Methodology." *Practicing Research in Writing Studies: Reflexive and Ethically Responsible Research.* Ed. Katrina M. Powell and Pamela Takayoshi. New York: Hampton P, 2012. 123–40. Print.

Smith, Dorothy. *Institutional Ethnography as Practice.* Lanham: Rowman & Littlefield, 2006. Print.

—. *Institutional Ethnography: A Sociology for the People.* Lanham: AltaMira P, 2005. Print.

Strauss, Anselm, and Juliet Corbin. *Basics of Qualitative Research: Grounded Theory Procedures and Techniques.* Newbury Park: Sage, 1990. Print.

Townsend, Elizabeth. "Institutional Ethnography: A Method for Showing How Context Shapes Practice." *The Occupational Therapy Journal of Research* 16.3 (1996): 179–99. Print.

Head, Alison. "Unraveling the Citation Trail." *Project Information Literacy Smart Talk,* no. 8, Sandra Jamieson and Rebecca Moore Howard. The Citation Project, 15 Aug. 2011.

"WPA Outcomes Statement." (Version 2.0) Council of Writing Program Administrators. July 2008. Council of Writing Program Administrators. Web. 10 Aug. 2013.

Wardle, Elizabeth. "'Mutt Genres' and the Goal of FYC: Can We Help Students Write the Genres of the University?" *College Composition and Communication* 60.4 (2009): 765–88. Print.

ACKNOWLEDGMENTS

Many thanks to readers of early drafts of this project: E. Shelley Reid, Anicca Cox, Anne Beaufort, and Melissa Nicolas. This project was generously supported by a 2011 CWPA research grant.

Michelle LaFrance is assistant professor of English and director of the Writing Across the Curriculum program at George Mason University, a large research university. Her ethnographic research explores the take up of classroom practices in relation to local materialities and institutional discourses. She has published on institutional ethnography, writing centers, peer review, and the material conditions of writing programs.

Travelogue

Aspen and Honeysuckle: How Faculty Development for Teaching Writing Grows (Interview with Jessie Moore and Chris Anson)

Shirley K Rose

Shirley Rose [SR]: Chris and Jessie, thank you so much for taking time to talk with me about hosting the upcoming CWPA Summer Conference in Raleigh, North Carolina, on behalf of the Carolinas WPA regional affiliate organization and your respective home institutions, North Carolina State University and Elon University. This interview is the sixth in a series *WPA: Writing Program Administration* has devoted to conversations about the writing programs at the home institutions of the WPAs who serve as local hosts for the summer conference of the Council of Writing Program Administrators. I appreciate this chance to learn more about the Carolinas WPA and about the writing programs at your universities. I was surprised to learn that the Carolinas WPA, a regional affiliate of the Council of Writing Program Administrators, has two meetings a year. What happens at these meetings that makes WPAs from all over North and South Carolina willing, able, and eager to spend time together?

Chris Anson [CA]: Well, I know, Jessie is maybe a little more involved in the Carolinas WPA Affiliate than I am. I've done a couple of things for the group, but not very recently. But, I'll just tell you a little bit about one of the meetings. Jessie, it still takes place at Wildacres, right?

Jessie Moore [JM]: Yes, it does.

CA: Wildacres is a retreat center in a place called Little Switzerland, North Carolina, and it's up in the Blue Ridge Mountains. It's pretty isolated, with a whole bunch of switchbacks on the way there. The setting is stunning. Absolutely beautiful. The retreat center has communal dining in a beautiful dining hall area, and accommodations are somewhere between a dorm and a hotel. There is very limited access to technology. There is a phone booth because the cell phone connection can be a little bit dodgy at times. And the Internet, unless they've changed it, is of the sort that when they run out of bandwidth, they've run out. It is isolated. The whole idea is that you'll spend time with people there. There are some meeting rooms. There is a really comfortable lodge with a huge fireplace and overstuffed chairs.

The Wildacres retreat center was used many years ago by UNC Charlotte as a retreat to support their writing across the curriculum efforts. That use eventually fizzled out, but then the site was picked up by the Carolinas WPA, as the site where the once-a-year meetings should take place. Jessie, would we consider that the main meeting?

JM: Not necessarily the main meeting, but the September meeting.

CA: The September meeting, right. So, that's one of the contexts where WPAs get together. We've had people from other states, who were not part of the Carolinas, join. It's a great place to have meetings and presentations. There is a bigger venue that's like a little auditorium. And it's also a great place for people just to mingle. There are always activities in the evening.

SR: Are you saying that you have a sense that the setting itself for that September meeting is part of the draw of the Carolina WPA meetings?

JM: Absolutely.

CA: It's part of the draw, but it's also part of what happens. The setting and the sort of mini-conference are really closely connected because the setting allows for the kind of talk and sharing that happens at any conference but especially because you're all together. You're in a beautiful setting. It's designed to be a retreat center where there is nowhere else to go. You have to drive down the mountain to get anywhere near civilization, so you're there with all the other people just sharing and communing. It's a really special place.

SR: Jessie, could you talk a little bit about some of the specific activities or thematic emphases— either a recent one or the one that is coming up—so I can get an idea of what kind of things happen?

JM: The board explicitly tries to make the September meeting at Wildacres very retreat-oriented; so one year, I think it was probably two or three years ago, we invited Dave Blakesley to come up from Clemson in South Carolina and offer strategies for publishing about writing program research. We organized the day so that after his opening keynote, people had time to write; they had time to get feedback; they had time to meet one-on-one with Dave—time to work together, time to work individually, time to get feedback from someone who has expertise. And there was downtime as well—time to really enjoy the hiking trails, to socialize with other WPAs. There is a canteen onsite, so we always bring food and wine and beer and sodas so that folks can just mingle and enjoy each other's company. But the canteen is also a space where the conversations continue into the evening.

John Warner was our guest last year, and the focus topic was looking at some of the working conditions within our field and working together to think about how at our own institutions we could make small changes or work towards larger changes. We had one a couple years ago that was on grants and finding and applying for grant opportunities. We had one on assessment. But, again, all of these are set up with the idea that there is time to learn some new strategies, time to put them into practice, time to get feedback, and then downtime to rejuvenate as well.

SR: Those sound like great programs. They are filling a need thematically, but also they offer a chance to spend time with other people who have the same issues and can also help you not just problem solve but maybe be part of your solution. That sounds great. Tell me what typically happens at the other meeting that you have each year?

JM: The Meeting in the Middle is held each February except for the occasional times when snow interrupts the plans, and we have to postpone until May. It is usually held in February as the chronological meeting in the middle between the September retreats but also the geographic meeting in the middle between North Carolina and South Carolina. We meet at the UNC Charlotte Center City Building, which is a great space. It always seems a little underutilized, but it's got really nice and flexible classroom spaces. It has a library outpost, and then it always has things like art exhibits as well. It's a space where what we do is a bit more focused. We are only together for a day. Typically, in the morning we will have a presentation—whether it is on a new advancement in the field, a new issue that has come up, or something that there is local expertise on to share. Then in the afternoon, we do one of two things: Some years we have poster sessions where people can share research in progress and get feedback on it. Some years we have discussion leaders where people come with questions that they're working through and share how they've approached those questions or challenges or opportunities so far and then open up and facilitate discussion in small groups about those topics. So, it is still very much centered on community. For both of these events, we try to elicit expertise or draw on expertise from within the Carolinas. The Meeting in the Middle serves a couple purposes. It is the touch point in the middle of the year; it is the middle of the academic year, bringing us together as a group but also trying to help us work through issues we're facing. And, it is a space where it's a little easier to bring graduate students and even undergraduates. Graduate students also come to the September conference at Wildacres, but because Meeting in the Middle is so short, it is just a day, it is easier for undergraduates for instance to attend.

SR: I'm fascinated with the ways you're describing that these spaces contribute to the substance. They structure what you're doing, and they also contribute to the content and the substance of the meetings.

CA: Although we cover South and North Carolina, North Carolina has a large, many-campus state system. So even though we're all doing somewhat different things across our campuses, we're all part of the same system, and therefore we're sometimes talking about issues that are coming from the system office, which is in Chapel Hill. Seventeen campuses are organized under the UNC System, not including many community colleges that are also state supported. So I think people crave the opportunity to get together with other UNC System colleagues and talk. But, then we also have so many other universities such as Elon and Duke and others that also participate.

JM: When the organization started, Meg Morgan and Marsha Lee-Baker started it as a gathering of members of the UNC System, but at the point that the affiliate submitted its proposal for affiliate status, Elon had signed on as an initial member outside of the system, and there were a lot of shared interests and challenges and opportunities even beyond the state system.

SR: There have been and currently are numerous CWPA affiliate organizations. Some are regional, like the Carolinas WPA, and some have been organized around similarities of institutional type. I know for a while there was a discussion of an affiliate for Jesuit schools. How does the Carolinas WPA reflect the geographical region that you are all from? What makes it the Carolinas WPA?

JM: I think part of it is drawing from the systems, but we're very attentive to the regional expertise and trying to build that local network. A couple board members were working last week on trying to fill in some blanks on a regional directory of WPAs in North Carolina and South Carolina, and one of the things that we're feeling is that certainly the WPAs who are in state systems really need that support structure of being able to touch base with other WPAs in the system and see what's happening, how they are applying different policies, how they're being impacted by different state policies but then also recognizing that there is expertise within the region that we can draw on when we have questions, when we need an outside consultant, those kinds of things, so trying to look to the expertise that is developing within the two Carolinas and tap that and showcase it and really celebrate it.

SR: That makes a lot of sense.

CA: I think there was a strong orientation, as Jessie pointed out, toward North Carolina, and then I don't know why we didn't look to Virginia, but my sense is there are other things going on in that area. We didn't want to go too far geographically.

JM: With our Meeting in the Middle, part of the reason we meet in Charlotte is that it is a location that pretty much anywhere you are in North Carolina or South Carolina, it is not more than a four-hour drive. While the September meeting has been at Wildacres for several years, the organization experimented with alternating between Wildacres and a coastal location in South Carolina, and the South Carolina options were a little too expensive and a little too restrictive, so we've ended up coming back consistently to Wildacres.

SR: The 2016 CWPA summer conference theme, Engaging Multiple Perspectives in and about Writing Program Administration, seems very well suited to a conference that is hosted by two different universities and a regional affiliate WPA organization. How does that conference theme reflect values and aspirations of your home institutions and of the Carolinas WPAs?

JM: I think for me speaking in terms of Elon, and also I think in terms of Carolinas WPA the multiple perspectives resonates because in Carolinas WPA, we've worked to be sure that we're inclusive of all types of writing programs. We certainly have first-year writing programs represented and writing centers and writing across the curriculum or writing in the disciplines, but then we also have things like writing majors and writing minors. So, serving as a reminder that those are additional types of writing program administrations that can be represented in our conversations as WPAs. They may not have all of the same questions and same challenges, but they do have some carry over, some overlap. Inclusivity has been important to Carolinas WPA and also reflective of Elon's writing programs. The folks that have the longest history in the Elon writing programs have moved across the different programs in the institution. They've picked up multiple perspectives along the way, but then those multiple perspectives have also informed how they've mentored junior WPAs at the institution.

SR: That seems really important, Jessie. It does seem important, how you're characterizing the people at Elon as having had leadership roles in different writing programs, different parts of the program, so that they know what the issues are, and there is some shared disciplinary expertise.

JM: Absolutely. Just as a couple quick examples. Tim Peeples was hired here to work on WAC and the writing center, and he's since moved into upper level administration, but he certainly still draws on that WAC and writing center experience and worked with others here to start our professional writing and rhetoric concentration. My colleague Paula Rosinski was the first-year writing program coordinator when I came, and she rotated into the writing center and, most recently, she's been identified as the Writing Across the University director.

SR: Chris, what would you add about the Carolinas WPA and your own institution, North Carolina State University, reflecting the values expressed in the conference theme?

CA: I was going to echo what Jessie said about the CWPA and the universities in the region because they are so different. We have big flagships, we have mid-size universities, private universities. We have small liberal arts colleges like Davidson. We have a number of HBCUs, some of them state supported like NCA&T, others private like Bennett College, which is a small women's college in Greensboro. Mid-size regional campuses are almost like flagships. They've grown so much, like UNC Charlotte. So I think there is a great range of writing programs represented in all these different campuses. And of course, the ones in South Carolina, such as Clemson. We don't have as much community college involvement as any of us would like. We have a huge community college system here with a range of focuses. I would say just briefly about that theme that the NC State writing program tries to mirror the emphasis on writing across the curriculum and writing in the disciplines. It's always looking outward at other contexts. The actual pedagogy or the nature of the curriculum in the first-year writing program is WAC-oriented, and the program that I direct works with faculty across the whole university on both writing and oral communication. Our College of Humanities and Social Sciences is more likely to be reflective about writing, yet we have other colleges where there is a strong emphasis on preparing students for the kinds of work that they'll be doing. So there is a diverse set of interests in the way writing should work. It goes with that theme effectively.

SR: My next few questions are specific to each of your institutions, so I'm going to start with Jessie, and Chris, if you don't mind my focusing on Jessie, maybe chip in with a question of your own for her or any comment that you want to make, but we'll have the focus on Elon and then move to NC State.

Jessie, in my research about Elon, I found that Elon was named one of the nation's top three universities for community service in President Bush's inaugural higher education service honor roll. How are Elon's writing programs engaged in meeting the university's commitment to community service?

JM: That's a great question. The levels of involvement have varied in different years, but a couple things that have been consistent: Our professional writing and rhetoric concentration in the English major and our professional writing studies minor both routinely include service learning courses. Those are actually designated courses that fulfill an experiential learning requirement for students, but students in those courses end up partnering with local agencies and doing writing projects in collaboration with those agencies. They've done things like research for a conservators' center that's near campus, figuring out what was bringing people back, what kinds of things would inspire people to make donations, doing research on what sort of things people would be willing to buy in a gift shop, those types of things, and then making recommendations, and even creating some books about the conservators' center for the organization to sell in their gift store. That's just one example, but we have a lot of those types of course-based partnerships with community partners that contribute to that service hour count but also bring it back to the learning outcomes that are associated with the classes as well. The other example I have is that the writing center is very committed to offering its services to the local community, and that can take the form of community members coming in with resumes or other documents that they were hoping to get feedback on. Writing Center consultants also visit local elementary schools to offer writing workshop-type programs in the schools, both the one that is literally a block away from the university and ones that are in other parts of the larger Alamance-Burlington area.

SR: That leads me into the next question—at least I'm seeing a connection. How do Elon University and its writing programs reflect the regional location? I'm asking a question about place.

JM: It took me a while to think about how I wanted to answer that question because on one hand if you walk on to Elon's campus, it is an officially recognized botanical garden. It's a gorgeous campus, but that beauty itself does not necessarily set it apart from our peer and aspirant institutions. It's what we do with our spaces that helps anchor us in North Carolina and some of the community projects that we do through service learning. But then we also as a campus have made a commitment to trying to break down the town-gown division, so we have for instance a downtown space that we use for some K-12 education programs and volunteer opportunities at the library and other things like that. We're trying to bridge beyond our campus into spaces that are town spaces that town members want to become thriving areas. We're thinking about what needs we can address in those spaces. We also have a service-learning center called the Kernodle Center for Service Learning. Students take responsibility for being volunteer leads with different organizations within the community. I'm not going to remember all of the sites, but Boys and Girls Club is one. So, these students figure out, in collaboration with the community partner, what the volunteer needs are there and then work to get volunteers from campus to the organization programs. There's a lot of attention to not just going out and doing what we think is needed but working in collaboration with our community partners to figure out what their needs are and to negotiate which of those needs we can meet and to admit which ones we can't necessarily meet at this time but that we can keep in mind as we are moving forward with other courses and other programs.

The other thing that I was thinking about is a more physical thing and also a cultural thing. You would know that you're at Elon because there are colonnades on lots of the buildings, so it's a very Elon look. You could sit someone down on several different parts of campus and they would know that it was part of Elon.

SR: There's an architectural motif that is repeated in all of the buildings?

JM: Yes. Lots of red brick, lots of red brick pathways in addition to the red brick in the buildings. And then there are colonnades connecting a lot of the buildings and neighborhoods. My office, for instance, is in the Academic Pavilion neighborhood, and there are, let's see, six pavilions and an anchor building where you could walk from building to building to building under the colonnades and never have to go outside the colonnades.

SR: What's the reason for that? Is that an attempt to invoke a particular feel or identity for the school?

JM: Part of it is. The campus had a fire in 1923, and it destroyed all of the campus except, if I remember correctly, one building, and so the buildings that have been constructed since then really emulate that surviving building and carry that architectural look across campus. But then there is also the practical reason that, in the summer it gets really hot, so the colonnades that connect the buildings offer some shade if you're walking from building to building. When we have rain, they can also offer some cover if you're walking among the buildings.

SR: Elon was founded, I read, as a Christian college in the late 19th century. Do you see any of those origins still evident?

JM: We do a bit. The Christian Church that was the founding organization later became part of the United Church of Christ, and we ended our formal affiliation with the United Church of Christ, I think, about three or four years ago, but we in our mission still talk about embracing the founders' vision of an academic community that transforms mind, body, and spirit and encourages freedom of thought and liberty of conscious. We have become more inclusive and encompassing in how we see that nurtured spirit but—the mind, body, and spirit—we haven't lost that spirit piece. Now it's supported through things like a multi-faith center that hosts both multi-faith and inter-faith events. We also have some non-denominational activities that focus on spirituality and wellness and well-being, so that piece is still evident. And then one way that I think is a little surprising to new faculty is we still have an invocation at the start of each faculty meeting, and if you go to formal gatherings in the evening on campus, there is often an invocation at the start of those as well. It's become much more multi-faith in its representation, but there's still a tradition on our campus.

SR: My next question is about you. You're currently the Associate Director for the Center for Engaged Learning. Having worked with you at Purdue during your PhD program and having seen your work as a mentor for new teachers of writing, I'm not surprised that you're now providing leadership for that center. What was the path that led you to that role?

JM: When I was in my second year here, I temporarily filled in as the writing program administrator for the first-year writing program, and within the next year that became a permanent position in as much as any of our positions are permanent. I held that role for about five years, and one of the things that I enjoyed in that role was that, in addition to handling a lot of the traditional administrative tasks that we think of in writing programs, I had a lot of flexibility over how I approached faculty development, and I had a fair amount of buy-in for faculty development. So, I wanted in that space to push the envelope a little bit and invite my colleagues, many of whom are trained in literature or trained in creative writing or other areas, to engage in some of the programmatic research and assessment research as a way to help them learn more about the field and about how to teach first-year writing. We had two research projects that worked pretty well in terms of both meeting the goal of engaging colleagues in the work of the writing program but also helping develop local data that could address questions about why we do things the way we do or why we would recommend certain practices for the writing program. That experience led to discussions about what would a larger research project look like that built on that idea of collaborative research, and eventually—with Tim Peeples and Peter Felten—we came up with the concept of the Elon Research Seminar on Writing Transfer, considering the question of transfer, which of course we also invited Chris to be a fellow seminar leader for. That work then gave me experience working with multi-institutional teams and providing leadership on scholarship of teaching and learning projects that moved beyond a single institution. Because of the success of that experience, we wanted as an institution to pursue additional research on high-impact pedagogies and engaged learning. Knowing that we are well known for students' opportunities to participate in high-impact pedagogies, we wanted to contribute more to research about them, and so that opened up an opportunity for me to step into the leadership role at the Center for Engaged Learning where that's my primary responsibility—facilitating, guiding, and providing leadership for these multi-institutional research projects.

SR: I see how that is very connected to your work with the Carolinas WPAs, too, with the cross-institutional networking involved.

JM: Absolutely.

SR: One last question for you, Jessie. I have a metaphor for the program I direct, which is the writing program here at Arizona State University, and that metaphor is the ocotillo. I don't know if you've ever seen one, but it grows very tall. It is a plant that is native to the desert Southwest, and it can survive on very little water. When it has to do that, it is straggly and dead looking. It just looks like sticks. But, when it gets water, it has thousands of tiny leaves on each branch and bright red flowers at the tips. It's stunning. I think of my writing program as the same. We can get by, we can survive on really minimal resources, though we will appear to be dead, and we will be scary looking. However, when we get the resources we need, we can be stunning and can do amazing things. Do you have a metaphor for the Center for Engaged Learning, which you direct?

JM: I tend to think of it like a grove of aspen trees, and it is not so much just what you see on the surface with the cluster of aspen together but what's happening underneath where you've got the roots creating a rhizomatic structure. Our center is hosting its fifth research seminar this summer; we've got several clusters of aspen groves scattered around and about where we are fostering strong connections around their topics, but then we are also the root system connecting each of those, so you can't really tell where one ends and one begins. It is both our research programs and the way that they are linked but also the network of people who are involved and how they become linked.

SR: That's a very nice metaphor.

JM: Thank you, I like yours.

SR: Thank you, Jessie. I'm going to move to questions for Chris. If you think of more you want to say, jump in. If you think of questions you have for Chris or comments you want to make on his responses, please feel free to do that.

Chris, most academics are aware of the significance of the Research Triangle that is made up of the University of North Carolina, Duke University, and North Carolina State University and the influence and outcomes that that collaboration, which started in the 1950s has had. How has NC State's participation in the Research Triangle influenced its culture of writing and writing instruction?

CA: In the middle of that triangle of universities is what's called the Research Triangle Park, and that consists of 170 mostly research and development companies that are heavily involved in research in all sorts of high tech areas. There is an EPA facility there. The location was, as you pointed out, set up very wisely, given what's happened to other industries in the state, such as tobacco and furniture making. I think that's had a big influence because many students want to stay in the state. In turn, the state wants students who are educated here to stay here and then put all their new knowledge to work bettering the state. I think we're considered a very high-powered research area, and that works well in tandem with the goals and mission of NC State University—all the universities for that matter—but especially NC State because it's got such strong ties as a land grant to the state itself, with major agricultural programs and high-tech majors. We've seen a lot of collaboration, not only among the universities, but especially between the universities and private businesses and corporations and research and development companies in the area that are engaged in nanotechnology and pharmaceuticals and other kinds of research. The other thing I might mention is that North Carolina State created a second campus that's very close to the main campus. It's less than a mile and was supposed to be connected with a monorail that has yet to be built. It's called the Centennial Campus, and it's a collaboration between NC State University, the state of North Carolina, and private industries. The industries have been putting up money to build research facilities on this land. Alongside those and mixed into them are NC State University buildings. So graduate students will go and work with people in these industries, and the industry people will work with faculty. The whole idea is to get collaboration going between these obviously very educated, skilled researchers on the campus and these very educated and skilled researchers in industry, which makes the level of PhDs in the Triangle among the highest in the US. It's a very smart area because so many people have advanced degrees in order to work in these industries.

SR: Yes. I can see that.

CA: I think NC State is in a good position to work alongside people who are innovating and developing new ideas and products. Because the state likes students to go work elsewhere in the state, I think we at NC State become feeders to those industries. When we talk to the people in area companies, they tell us over and over again that even more than content knowledge, they want three things: They want good writing skills, they want good oral communication skills, and they want good skills in teamwork because everybody works in teams. In a lot of ways, that drives the university's focus on communication. They find it so important that we have to hear that message, and I think people in other departments and other colleges hear it as well, so that has made our lives a little bit easier. In my life as a WAC director, it's not hard for me to convince faculty elsewhere of the importance of these abilities because everybody that they're connected to is saying they want them.

SR: I'm going to say back what I think I'm hearing from you. You're saying that because there are these companies—the Research Triangle Park and the Centennial Campus, which is like an incubator for these companies—the geographical location reflects how closely connected these groups are with the university as we might usually think of it, that is as just faculty and students—faculty and students doing research. Those close connections mean that the faculty are very aware of what the work place is really requiring.

CA: Yes, it's what the students in those majors are going to be doing if they want to work in these industries. You know, not all of them want to go away, far away. There are others who are not sure if they are going to go to grad school or do other things. There is a strong emphasis on the relationship between the research that goes on, particularly in the Triangle, and what we're doing with the students. As I said, that comes back to influence us in terms of the emphasis on writing.

SR: You anticipated this question a little bit, but I'm going to go ahead and ask it because I want to see what more you might have to say. NC State is a land grant institution. Do you think the original values that contributed to the establishment of the land grant colleges and universities in the 19th century are evident in the way the campus Writing and Speaking Program has and is developing in the 21st century? I think there is maybe a missing middle in there about whether the land grant mission is still central to NC State and how your program may embody that.

CA: I think the first part of that is yes, especially in the agricultural areas and maybe in the College of Textiles, which is highly ranked, and this has been a major area for the development of the textiles industry. But now it's all extraordinarily high tech. You know, it's textiles chemistry. It's not weaving and looms and all that. It's NASA space suits, bacteria-free socks.

SR: Invisibility cloaks [laughter].

CA: All that kind of stuff. It's very high tech. So I think it's morphed a lot. It's developed and changed over the years. But I think there is still a strong emphasis, at NC State maybe more than the other UNC campuses, on the relationship between what we're doing and what the state's needs are, particularly felt in the area of agricultural research, textiles, engineering, and some other areas. The thing that you should know about the UNC System is that the system office doesn't like duplication of effort. So if you look at UNC Chapel Hill, our sister campus, you'll see that they have a law school. We don't. They have a medical school. We have a highly-ranked vet school. We do engineering. They don't. We're a special university, and they're a special university. That's true for our Communication, Rhetoric, and Digital Media PhD, which is just a few years old. When we created that, we could not create a typical rhet-comp program. It had to be something that did not exist elsewhere. Because we're a high tech institution, we thought the digital media component would serve those interests well, and it has. I think those values are still there; they've just developed along new lines.

SR: That makes a lot of sense related to writing programs. If WPA summer conference attendees were to visit the campus of North Carolina State University, which from the map looks like it is just a few miles from the conference hotel, maybe even walking distance, what would you recommend that they see, other than your office or offices related to Writing Programs? What would you recommend that they see that would help them understand the ways in which the university and its writing programs are culturally located?

CA: I think they should go to the Centennial Campus and look at the new library there, the Hunt Library. It was built for that part of the campus, and it's perhaps the most futuristic library in the world. It's stunning. Little kids get bused in from the schools just to see it. Architecturally, it's striking, and then once you're inside, it's compelling. Completely robotically controlled, so—and I don't know if I like this that much—you never have to be in a stack. The stacks are all there, and they go up several stories, and you can watch books being retrieved by robotic mechanisms.

JM: It's a little hard to browse the stacks.

CA: They have a browsing system on the computer that shows what else is contiguous. I'm not sure if that satisfies my need to walk around and pull books off the shelf, but it's a really amazing building, and it's worth visiting.

SR: How far away from the hotel is that?

CA: I'd say it is a couple of miles, not walking distance, but it's not too far.

JM: There is a good bus system.

SR: I want to ask this question that is about you. We've known each other since 1984, and that's most of my academic career, but we got to know each other a little better during the years that we were going through the presidential rotation for WPA, which of course involves conference planning. How has planning a WPA summer conference as a local host been different from planning for a conference as a WPA president?

CA: For me, the big difference is that I'm not working on the content of the program. Susan [Miller-Cochran] as CWPA President is in charge of putting together the conference itself. So this represents a real change for me because as president, I was not worrying about the local arrangements. And that's what Jessie and I are now working on. It's really a pleasure in a lot of ways to think about people's experiences beyond what will happen in the hallways and rooms of the conference. What else is around? What is in Raleigh? What can we do to highlight what is here and available? And that's been really fun to work on with the help, of course, of many other people, including Jessie who has been our lead person.

SR: That's part of what I want to be bringing out in this travelogue. What do you want people who come for the conference to have an experience of so that they understand place?

JM: If I can jump in really quick on that, one of the things that Chris has been taking the lead on with graduate students at NC State is the Saturday social. They came up with the idea of having a North Carolina barbeque competition of sorts, so folks can see and taste the difference between eastern style and western style North Carolina barbeque.

SR: That sounds great. I have one last question for you, Chris. What is your metaphor for your writing program?

CA: To continue with the plant metaphors, I think I would have to say the honeysuckle, and I'll tell you why. First of all, I think, because I direct a writing across the curriculum program or writing and speaking across the curriculum program, I'm always hopeful that what we do kind of creeps into and entwines different programs and curriculums here. So that's one thing—honeysuckle creeps around and gets into places. The second thing is, it's interesting because it kind of grows vertically as well as horizontally, and we're finding ourselves moving not just across the curriculum but into its upper reaches. Increasingly, there are calls for more attention to graduate education; the honeysuckle goes up as well as out, and that's a suitable metaphor for how we're looking into the highest levels of the major and maybe graduate education. Originally I was thinking of kudzu, but that tends to smother what it covers and choke it out. The honeysuckle has tendrils that move in, but they don't take over. They don't dominate what they're moving into, and that's very important for us because we don't want to smother what people do. We want to provide them with some support and then let it grow from there—adorn it but also put down a few roots. Honeysuckle smells sweet. I hope that we leave something behind that is attractive. I think that if you really wanted to extend the metaphor, it also attracts things like hummingbirds and bees, and those become propagators. Hummingbirds help propagate more honeysuckles, so the whole environment of them leads to the spread of the ideas about writing and speaking.

SR: That's great.

CA: And also for the first-year writing program because that's also a writing across the curriculum-oriented program.

SR: Do you have other things you want to say?

JM: It's been a fun opportunity to collaborate with another institution and with the Carolinas WPA so that we can take advantage of regional expertise. On the website, we're going to be adding pages on things to do not only in Raleigh but in the Carolinas, and that kind of addition would be harder to do without that state expertise.

CA: Maybe also, just to add to that the notion of diversity topographically, that if people wanted to do more here, if they go west, they're going to be in the Blue Ridge and from there into the Smokies. If they go east, they can be down in Wilmington, where there are some barrier islands, or they can go to the Outer Banks. If they like golf, they can go to Pinehurst. There is a lot of diversity topographically for vacations in the area.

SR: One last question that I know WPA journal readers and summer conference attendees have: In this past March (2016), the North Carolina state legislature passed House Bill 2 rescinding all local LGBT-inclusive nondiscrimination policies throughout the state. By the time this interview is published, the law may have been struck down; but at this time, what are your plans for providing information about the situation and supporting any activist work in which conference attendees might want to participate?

JM: We plan to invite local LGBTQIA groups to share materials and resources at an exhibit table, we'll host the Workshop dinner at a restaurant that is on the Safe Bathrooms list, and we'll facilitate an opportunity for civic action for participants seeking a way to engage more extensively in supporting the local and disciplinary LGBTQIA community. We're following the lawsuits and corporate responses carefully so that we can continue to adjust our plans as we move forward; we hope CWPA members will join us in North Carolina to participate in the existing conference traditions and also to join us in civic action in support of our LGBTQIA colleagues and friends.

SR: Thank you to both of you for all you are doing to thoughtfully address this issue as the situation evolves and to keep CWPA members informed about plans for action at the conference as they develop over the next few months. And thanks for talking with me about writing programs at your institutions and about the Carolinas WPA.

JM: Thank you.

CA: Thank you.

Review

A New Perspective on Language-Level Writing Instruction

Anne Ruggles Gere

Aull, Laura. *First-Year University Writing: A Corpus-Based Study with Implications for Pedagogy.* New York: Palgrave Macmillan, 2015. Print. 239 pages.

The relationship between composition studies and language-level approaches to writing instruction has a tortured history. Institutional dealings between departments of linguistics and English studies (where most research on and teaching of writing emerged) have been fraught since the two areas of study emerged. As composition and rhetoric began to take shape as a field, language-level strategies like sentence-combining, tagmemics (Young, Becker, and Pike), and generative rhetoric of the sentence (Christensen) flourished briefly and then vanished under the weight of the growing emphasis on process-focused writing (Emig; Murray) and the somewhat later attention to cognitive approaches (Bereiter and Scardamalia; Flower and Hayes). Theoretical developments in the field of linguistics and attention to ideal—rather than actual—users of language also made it more difficult to incorporate language-level approaches into composition studies. Still, some scholars, particularly those who work with English language learners and speakers of dialects such as African American Vernacular, have continued to advocate for a rapprochement between the two areas. Laura Aull's ground-breaking book offers a promising new direction for achieving genuine collaboration. More importantly, it provides innovative and highly useful strategies for teaching first-year students.

    A mixture of the theoretical, empirical, and pedagogical, this book attends to the needs of students in first-year writing (FYW) courses, noting that they can benefit from understanding academic conventions and considering "how to foster students' awareness of how language-level patterns contribute to the success or failure of written academic texts" (12). Aull surveys the landscape of FYW and its general lack of attention to language-level instruction and traces the history of the relationship between linguistics and composition. She concludes this survey of the past by offering genre studies as a space where language-level approaches and composition studies can come together. Her rationale is based on recent genre study in both fields where language-level tools have been used to deepen understanding of patterns in academic writing.

Genre studies in linguistics has included analysis of recurring moves in the introductions to research articles. These moves include establishing a territory, creating a niche in that territory, and occupying the niche (Swales). Move analysis such as this is accomplished through reading multiple texts and identifying patterns that emerge. Another tool of genre studies in linguistics is the automated text analysis, the computer-aided identification of specific words and phrases in a corpus or collection of thousands of texts. This form of analysis can identify in quantitative terms commonly used words, or lexical items, as well as collocations, or the words that surround them. This capacity makes it possible to discern recurring patterns of words and phrases that appear in written texts, whether those of students or academic specialists. Such analysis can be used to determine language-level differences between writing produced by varied groups of students or between students and professional writers. Features such as hedging or qualifying language, boosters or intensifying language, personal pronouns, transitional words, and reformulations have been used in linguistics-based genre studies to describe varying abilities of student writers, to compare their writing to that of academic specialists in their field of study, and to identify differences between writers in various disciplines (Hyland; Lancaster; Aull and Lancaster). Computers' ability to identify specific words and phrases in thousands of texts illuminates patterns that usually remain invisible to individual instructors.

Rhetorical genre studies, the other approach Aull discusses, is more familiar to compositionists via the work of Carolyn Miller, David Russell, Amy Devitt, and Anis Bawashi. Here, the emphasis is on whole-text rhetorical features such as context and audience along with the social actions that texts shape and are shaped by. Aull notes that this version of genre studies has not attended to language-level features, and she argues that bringing the two together in context-informed analysis of language features can yield information that will improve teaching and learning in FYW.

The most important part of Aull's book, then, is devoted to demonstrating what analysis that combines language-level and rhetorical genre studies looks like and how it can be used in FYW classes to demystify academic writing for students. After delineating the terms and tools of language-level analysis of student writing, including illustrations of computer-generated word lists, she describes her study of two collections, or corpora, of essays written by first-year students as part of a directed self-placement process. In the interest of full disclosure, I need to acknowledge that one of these collections was created by the directed self-placement process I instituted at the Sweetland Center for Writing at the University of Michigan; I shared it with Aull, my former student, but I had no role in this study or in any other aspect of her book. The other collection or corpus was drawn from the directed self-placement system Aull established at Wake Forest University.

As part of her contextual analysis of these two collections of student writing, Aull compares the two institutions, the circumstances of composing, and the prompts—all focused on evidence-based arguments—that were used in each case. Then she shows how she used computer-assisted analysis to examine the use of self-mentions in these two collections and to compare them with collections or corpora of writing from the Contemporary Corpus of American English, a source of expert writing (Davies). She summarizes the major findings of this analysis:

> (1) most FY writers use first person pronouns more than expert writers, regardless of whether personal evidence was solicited by the prompt, but even more frequently when it was; (2) the FY writers use first person pronouns to mark evidence in various ways, including ways that do not mirror how expert writers use them; (3) when the FY prompt both solicited personal evidence and posed an open-ended question—rather than inviting a direct response to a source text argument—the FY references to personal evidence are higher, and they appear to be at the expense of references to the source text or author. (62)

Aull usefully contextualizes these findings by showing, for example, how "I will" can be used to highlight personal experience in what she terms text-external markers (more common among students) or to draw attention to reasons or examples in the text which she calls text-internal markers (more common among experts). These distinctions show how a combination of language-level and composition studies analysis can yield information useful for composition instructors and their students. Similarly, she analyzes the relationships between prompts and students' varying use of self-references and, based on the differences she finds, observes that prompts that invite personal evidence or include open-ended questions are not the best way to help first-year students learn to write the effective evidence-based arguments required in many college classes.

Another dimension of Aull's analysis of these two collections of student writing focuses on issues of scope and certainty. Here she compares how students and more expert writers use words categorized as hedges (e.g., generally, possible, approximately) and boosters (certainly, decidedly, always). These features, along with text-internal markers and text-external markers, have both formal or language-level and rhetorical dimensions because they illuminate the rhetorical stance taken by writers as well as the means by which they construct that stance. Aull's finding that less able student writers use more boosters while more expert writers use a mixture of boosters and hedges may not be surprising, but both the claim and the solid empirical basis for it cast new light on the problems student writers encounter as they attempt to write evidence-based arguments. Instructors who criticize students for being too general may not be consciously aware of the patterns of boosters and text-external markers that underlie that critique. Likewise, students may be unaware of these features in their own writing just as (I have found) they are often surprised by their own over-use of *to be* verbs.

The larger issue raised by Aull's analysis of hedges and boosters centers on questions about epistemic commitment. Like many writing instructors, I lament the number of first-year writers who have not yet learned to distinguish between stating an opinion and making an argument. Aull suggests that students may not understand that an effective evidence-based argument calls upon the language of certainty and caution. She suggests:

> One way we might help clarify expectations of academic argumentation for students, then, is to discuss how writers balance certainty and possibility through patterns of hedges and boosters. Sharing findings like those in this analysis might be one way to do so, because they reflect three relevant trends: the value of tempered claims in academic writing, some features shared by FY writers that are not shared by expert writers, and some language-level options for constructing balanced arguments. (97)

I can imagine that making these features visible to students could help them understand the difference between stating an opinion and making an argument.

In addition to describing her analysis of student writing and suggesting instructional implications of her findings, Aull includes a chapter devoted to applications that instructors can take into their classrooms. One deals with hedges and boosters as markers of caution and certainty, explaining how they work, offering discussion questions, and providing examples of texts that can be shared with students. Aull's second pedagogical application focuses on markers of argumentative scope. She explains how text-internal, text-external, and personal evidence claims work, again including sample texts along with questions for discussion. Reformulation markers constitute the third application, and Aull shows how they reinterpret information or express it in a different way. Here too she includes questions for discussion along with texts that illustrate these markers. The final application centers on transition markers, and Aull includes the same apparatus of explanation, discussion questions, and sample texts. The detail included with each application makes it possible for instructors to take these materials directly into the classroom.

The last chapter in the book argues that making visible language-level features like the ones discussed here gives students access to discourses of power, especially because effective use of these features is often required in high-stakes writing assessment. Aull also assures her readers that attending to language-level features does not preclude considerations of context; the two can be complimentary, and attention to both does not require extensive training in linguistics.

While not every FYW course emphasizes the evidence-based argument, college writing does require students to be able to do this kind of writing. *First-Year University Writing* offers an innovative and accessible means of addressing some of the most challenging aspects of teaching students to write effective arguments. It offers clear demonstrations of how computer-assisted analysis can reveal patterns of language use that make real differences in writing. It shows how instructors can make these patterns visible to students. It offers hope that the long-standing differences between language-level and rhetorical approaches to writing can be redressed.

Works Cited

Aull, Laura, and Zak Lancaster. "Linguistic Markers of Stance in Early and Advanced Academic Writing: A Corpus-based Comparison." *Written Communication* 31.2 (2014): 151–83. Print.

Bawarshi, Anis. *Genre and the Invention of the Writer: Reconsidering the Place of Invention in Composition.* Logan: Utah State UP, 2003. Print.

Bereiter, Carl, and Marlene Scardamalia. *The Psychology of Written Communication.* Hillsdale: Erlbaum, 1987. Print.

Christensen, Francis. "A Generative Rhetoric of the Sentence." *College Composition and Communication* 14.3 (1963): 155–61. Print.

Davies, Mark. *The Contemporary Corpus of American English: 520 Million Words, 1990-Present.* 2008-Present. Web. 12 Dec. 2015.

Devitt, Amy. *Writing Genres.* Carbondale: Southern Illinois UP, 2004. Print.

Emig, Janet. *The Composing Processes of Twelfth Graders.* Urbana, IL: NCTE, 1971. Print.

Flower, Linda, and John R. Hayes. "A Cognitive Process Theory of Writing." *College Composition and Communication* 32.4 (1981) 365–87. Print.

Hyland, Kenneth. "Hedges, Boosters and Lexical Invisibility: Noticing Modifiers in Academic Texts." *Language Awareness* 9.4 (2000): 179–97. Print.

Lancaster, Zak. "Interpersonal Stance in L1 and L2 Students' Argumentative Writing in Economics: Implications for Faculty Development in WAC/WID Programs." *Across the Disciplines* 8.4 (2011). 21 Dec. 2011. Web. 3 Jan. 2016.

Miller, Carolyn. "Genre as Social Action." *Quarterly Journal of Speech* 70.2 (1984): 151–67. Print.

Murray, Donald. "Teach Writing as Process not Product." The Leaflet (Fall, 1972): 11–14. Rpt. in *The Essential Don Murray: Lessons from America's Greatest Writing Teacher*. Ed. Thomas Newkirk and Lisa C. Miller. Portsmouth: Boynton/Cook (2009): 1–5. Print.

Russell, David. "Activity Theory and Its Implications for Writing Instruction." *Reconceiving Writing, Rethinking Writing Instruction*. Ed. Joseph Petraglia. New York: Taylor and Francis, 1995. 51–78. Print.

Swales, John. *Genre Analysis: English in Academic and Research Settings*. Cambridge: Cambridge UP, 1990. Print.

Young, Richard, Alton L. Becker, and Kenneth L. Pike. *Rhetoric: Discovery and Change*. New York: Harcourt, 1970. Print.

Anne Ruggles Gere is Gertrude Buck Collegiate Professor and Arthur F. Thurnau Professor at the University of Michigan where she serves as Chair of the Joint PhD Program in English and Education and directs the Sweetland Center for Writing. A past chair of CCCC and a past president of NCTE, she is currently serving as Second Vice President of the Modern Language Association and will become President in 2018. She has published a dozen books and over seventy-five articles. Her current projects include a longitudinal study of student writing development across the undergraduate years and an investigation of the effects of integrating writing into large-enrollment gateway science courses.

Review

Writing Majors: Signs of Things to Come

T J Geiger II

Greg Giberson, Jim Nugent, and Lori Ostergaard, eds. *Writing Majors: Eighteen Program Profiles.* Logan: Utah State UP, 2015. Print. 266 pages.

Greg Giberson, Jim Nugent, and Lori Ostergaard's edited collection, *Writing Majors: Eighteen Program Profiles*, is a highly generative text. Here are just a few of the marginal comments I wrote on pages in this remarkable book as I read through it to prepare for writing this review: "Must share with committee members." "Cite in curriculum report." "Use for new course proposal." The chapters not only provide immediate help on a range of pressing programmatic and curricular issues; they've got me thinking, dreaming, believing—believing in writing faculty who organize for resources, in the value of trying something new, in rhetoric's reality-shaping power.

The appearance of *Writing Majors* signals the healthy, sustained growth of writing majors, and it spotlights important stories and insights for stakeholders creating or revising such programs. Fifteen years after the publication of *Coming of Age: The Advanced Writing Curriculum* and five years after *What We Are Becoming: Developments in the Undergraduate Writing Major, Writing Majors* speaks to the bold dreams and dogged labor of writing faculty who promote a wide-ranging and sophisticated vision of literacy education. In this regard, the field owes Giberson, who also co-edited *What We Are Becoming* with Thomas A. Moriarty, a debt for his sustained attention to writing majors. The editors of the new collection themselves "acknowledge a debt to *Composition Forum* for presenting the innovative series of writing program profiles that inspired" *Writing Majors* (6). In creating this collection, the editors not only draw attention to diverse profiles but also put them into conversation with one another.

This movement to think and represent writing majors in a holistic and programmatic way suggests something of a break with the history of what has been called advanced composition, a history that has haunted even recent efforts to imagine advanced instruction in writing. Much of the story of a course called advanced composition involves efforts to promote certain versions of a course (that is, celebrating its diverse manifestations) or to lament a lack of uniformity. Often, vivid descriptions of pedagogical moves within courses seemed intimations of authors' yearnings that their *enargia* become entelechies, organizing energies for structuring students' development. In *Writing Majors*, we bear witness to the writing major becoming a more powerful organizing force for thinking about postsecondary literacy education and that movement toward majors involves accounts of curricula that operate on broad bandwidths with lots of room for different kinds of courses to serve various outcomes.

One strength of this collection is its organizational scheme within the chapters, a point that Giberson discusses in his afterword. While some slight variation occasionally occurs, a shared structure organizes each chapter, enhancing the accessibility of the text and allowing for easier comparisons across programs. All chapters include an introduction, program overview and rationale, implementation narrative, reflection and prospection, and a curricular summary with major requirements. These chapters are arranged in two sections: programs in "writing departments" and programs in "English departments" (vi). While this section arrangement may place more emphasis on these traditional departmental distinctions than is strictly necessary, I still think readers will find the approach helpful, especially when trying to locate an institutional situation akin to their own. Rather than taking chapters or sections in their published order, I organize this review based on themes and issues that recur throughout the text and across chapters. While not every chapter receives a mention here, I recommend them all.

Institutional context, along with disciplinary and departmental negotiations, may well be the most oft-addressed concern. Some contributions indicate that a strong embrace of rhetoric as a liberal arts tradition (in keeping with a larger institutional mission) helps generate both an attractive practicality and a theoretically rich learning experience (Perron, Rist, and Loewe in chapter sixteen). How major programs are named indicates not only disciplinary affiliations but also practical and local issues (Grobman and Weisser in chapter fifteen). Names reflect, among other issues, a curriculum's focus, the concerns of faculty and institutions, and the need to attract students. Barbara E. L'Eplattenier and George H. Jensen (chapter two) discuss how disciplinary negotiation between writing studies and journalism historically influenced the writing major's shape at the University of Arkansas at Little Rock. Indeed, essentially every chapter helps readers imagine what organizing for a major might mean in a range of circumstances.

Negotiations—both local and disciplinary—unfold within the passage of time, and time—especially thinking in the long term—repeatedly surfaces as a concern in this collection. In an explicit way, Jessie L. Moore, Tim Peeples, Rebecca Pope-Ruark, and Paula Rosinski (chapter eighteen) invoke rhetorical notions of *chronos* and *kairos* as a way to theoretically imagine the unfolding process of writing major development. While some majors in the collection are long-established (the writing major at St. Edward's University dates to 1975), Sandra Jamieson's foreword helpfully reminds readers that, as a widespread disciplinary development, the writing "major is still in its infancy" (vii). As readers move through accounts that share stories of exciting work to create vibrant teaching and learning communities around writing, it's critical to keep the perspective Jamieson forwards and to think in the long term. As writing major programs exist for longer periods, faculty can turn to alumni to help understand the role writing and writing study play in former students' post-college lives. Laurie Grobman and Christian Weisser (chapter sixteen) demonstrate what this sort of long-term interest in students' lives might mean for program development.

The importance of locating potential allies and cultivating relationships emerges across several chapters. For example, administrative figures such as deans and provosts can be power brokers who make writing majors possible (Miles, Owens, and Pennell, chapter three; Smitherman, Mongno, and Payne, chapter five). Within a traditional English department, the goodwill of departmental colleagues can be critical to a major's success (Leverenz, Lucas, George, Hogg, and Murray, chapter eleven). Julie Dyke Ford, Julianne Newmark, and Rosário Durão (chapter nine) describe how, at a campus dedicated to science, technology, engineering, and mathematics fields, their department forged generative alliances not only on campus, but also within industry. Their department's corporate advisory board allowed for relationships to grow between academic faculty and professionals in industry and between students and potential employers. Grobman and Weisser (chapter fifteen) describe a similar advisory group of community members at Penn State Berks. I could easily imagine writing being marginalized or treated as purely instrumental in situations where literary studies dominate or where professional/technical writing serve as governing terms. However, the collection reflects a compelling diversity of programmatic and tactical responses based on specific local conditions and histories. While authors in this volume certainly don't seem to disregard the long history of writing's marginalization, this collection may suggest that dualisms that have historically shaped interactions between rhetoric and literature are not as important as they might once have been. Indeed, reconsidering long-standing commonplaces may be another shift that occurs as the field moves from its important focus on introductory writing courses and a few advanced courses toward writing majors.

As writing majors grow and spread, they will also interact with broader circular movements. For example, Zerbe and DelliCarpini note that the writing major at York College is "connecting professional aspirations with liberal learning" (128). They demonstrate how that connection serves not only their department, but also students more generally by discussing the writing major in relationship to general education and a first-year experience program. Undergraduate research opportunities also appear in this collection. Ford, Newmark, and Durão at New Mexico Tech note the importance of technical communication research activity in their curriculum. They also highlight, along with Grobman and Weisser, how undergraduate research publication and presentation opportunities contribute to students' learning. In short, authors demonstrate that the writing major never operates in isolation. Ideally, it works in a mutually supportive relationship with other sound teaching and programmatic practices. A writing major may, in fact, become a nexus or hub for developing many exciting opportunities for students, faculty, the university, and the broader community.

Pieces that take up the significance (or growing significance) of digital technology and media in writing major programs are numerous. As Nugent notes in the introduction, "Technology is vital" (5). Encouragement to embrace digital composing technologies runs throughout many chapters. At Columbia College, faculty came to a renewed focus on media, video, and journalism (Brinson and Tuten, chapter seventeen). The urgency around such issues is captured when L'Eplattenier and Jensen advertise that the department at the University of Arkansas at Little Rock "will focus on recruiting faculty who are skilled in new media" (30). Such growing attention to technology should surprise no one. Program planners should move forward intentionally to help students harness the power of 21st century composing technologies.

Writing Majors describes programs that promote specialized and professional expertise in ways that tend to blur the hard distinctions between disciplinary knowledge and teaching, between writing as practice and writing as declarative knowledge. In other words, writing majors point to the productive interaction of the pedagogical activities traditionally associated with writing studies' teaching focus and the discipline's academic professionalization through research activity. Heavily oriented toward the practical, the collection strikes me as the best of *praxis*: theoretically informed practice that encourages the field to think capaciously about students, to imagine undergraduate learning about writing as consequential intellectual work, and undergraduate writings as consequential material artifacts. In these chapters, students are positioned as disciplinary participants who grapple with complex knowledge, engage in research, compose for situated audiences, publish written work, showcase writing at local celebrations, and present at conferences. In this way, student learning and writing achieves consequences: feeding a discourse that argues affirmatively for the value of both writing pedagogy and writing students. Even as writing major programs are locally negotiated enterprises, differing in titles, courses, and emphases, they often allow students to work at the intersection of various realms of knowledge: writing studies, technical communication, literary studies, journalism, or creative writing.

Recent work speaks to how writing studies is at a point of recognizing what we are as a field and the content of our knowledge about writing. Such is the goal of *Naming What We Know: Threshold Concepts of Writing Studies* edited by Linda Adler-Kassner and Elizabeth Wardle. In *Writing Across Contexts: Transfer, Composition, and Sites of Writing*, Kathleen Blake Yancey, Liane Robertson, and Kara Taczak encourage us to think about how to enable students to write in ways that have consequences, that produce outcomes for the students, for audiences, for communities both local and distant. *Writing Majors* demonstrates that we have established programs of study that operationalize the concepts that we know.

As a whole, *Writing Majors* suggests at the disciplinary and major levels what WPAs know well at the program level and what instructors know at the classroom level: We can learn a lot from students. This learning informs our work. Classroom and program work might achieve effects that are small and local, but the work matters. As Giberson writes

> I do believe that these chapters taken collectively tell a story of a discipline that is *becoming* something, and that we are heading collectively in a particular direction, though not the direction that we as editors expected to find. . . . But it is exciting—and unsettling at times—and that is good. (247; emphasis original)

Amen.

Works Cited

Adler-Kassner, Linda, and Elizabeth Wardle, eds. *Naming What We Know: Threshold Concepts of Writing Studies*. Logan: Utah State UP, 2015. Print.

Giberson, Greg A., and Thomas A. Moriarty, eds. *What We Are Becoming: Developments in Undergraduate Writing Majors.* Logan: Utah State UP, 2010. Print.

Shamoon, Linda K., Rebecca Moore Howard, Sandra Jamieson, and Robert A. Schwegler, eds. *Coming of Age: The Advanced Writing Curriculum.* Portsmouth: Heinemann-Boynton/Cook, 2000. Print.

Yancey, Kathleen Blake, Liane Robertson, and Kara Taczak. *Writing Across Contexts: Transfer, Composition, and Sites of Writing.* Logan: Utah State UP, 2014. Print.

T J Geiger II is Assistant Professor of English at Lamar University. His research focuses on the writing major, writing studies pedagogy, and religious rhetoric. He has published work in College English, Composition Studies, Peitho, *and* CCTE Studies.

Review

Online Writing Instruction Principles and Practices: Now Is the Future

Elizabeth A. Monske

Hewett, Beth L., and Kevin Eric DePew, eds. *Foundational Practices of Online Writing Instruction*. Fort Collins, CO: WAC Clearinghouse and Parlor P, 2015. Print. 601 pages.

When the CCCC Committee for Effective Practices in Online Writing Instruction (OWI) released *A Position Statement of Principles and Example Effective Practices for Online Writing Instruction*, I was one of many in the CCCC 2013 standing room only session who desperately needed support from the national committee to inform discussions of pedagogical and technological resources; training and preparation for students and online writing instruction teachers; course caps; and relevance of OWI as a part of our research agendas at our institutions.

Formally released at the 2015 CCCC, *Foundational Practices of Online Writing Instruction* is another addition to the Perspectives on Writing Series through the WAC Clearinghouse and Parlor Press under the editorship of Susan H. McLeod. This collection is meant to ground the discussion in the committee's charge and the subsequent research the CCCC Committee for Effective Practices in OWI (referred to in both this collection and this review as the CCCC OWI Committee) to develop a consistent definition of online writing instruction (OWI) and the aforementioned position statement, whose principles drive each chapter. Each contributor to this collection has expertise in OWI and has contributed to or participated in the work of the CCCC OWI Committee. In their introduction, editors Beth L. Hewitt and Kevin Eric DePew note that "members are a diverse group of OWI educators and scholars: those who work for traditional and for-profit two- and four-year postsecondary institutions; specialists in multilingual writers, disabilities-based OWI, and other learning needs/ preferences; and online tutors and administrators" (5). The diversity of this group lends credibility and applicability for WPAs and faculty to discuss these issues with their varied institutional stakeholders.

This diverse group invites novice and veteran WPAs and OWI teachers into the important discussion by creating a common vocabulary and thorough explanations of the OWI Principles to engage with colleagues, WPAs, and administrators. Even with the breadth of the 600+ pages of this collection, by integrating the OWI principles and the chapters (even providing a cross-referencing chart of the principles to the corresponding chapter in the introduction), the collection shows cohesion and commitment to the mission of the CCCC OWI Committee and OWI Principle 1 that addresses accessibility and inclusivity.

The collection is broken down into five parts. Each section summarizes and provides key words to introduce each chapter. Notably, WPAs, specifically, are interlaced into many, if not all, of the discussions from this collection, which is important because they may be experiencing or will soon be confronted with issues of structuring opportunities to learn and develop new digital literacies, of the unification of efforts, and of understanding new learning structures and digital venues.

Introduction and Part I: An OWI Primer

The Introduction and the OWI Primer section cover much of the background and history of the CCCC OWI Committee and lay out the concerns and considerations for those developing a vision of coursework and programs online. The titles are indicative of the information found within each chapter. If readers are new to the OWI Principles or the CCCC OWI Committee and their work, Beth L. Hewitt (chapter one) fully develops each of the principles with a rational and in-depth discussion. Within the rationale and discussion, the differences and nuances of each principle are provided. Jason Snart (chapter two) covers the idea of hybrid or fully online OWI, while coverage of asynchronous and synchronous modalities is discussed in Connie Snyder Mick and Geoffrey Middlebrook's chapter (chapter three).

While many institutions may decide or implement the types of learning environments, both chapters two and three lend themselves to assisting WPAs or OWI teachers in understanding how to navigate, if not make, appropriate research-based decisions for OWI in terms of instructional goals, outcomes, and delivery for their programs. Specifically, Mick and Middlebrook advise WPAs to have discussions prioritized by OWI teacher experiences and encouragement of online classrooms spaces that support "online interconnectedness" rather than "simply technological feasibility," which is how an institution may make the decision (136). The authors then present a chart summarizing the strengths and challenges of asynchronous and synchronous modalities against three dimensions (inclusivity and accessibility; technical viability and IT support; and pedagogical rationale permanence, pace, scale, and social impact).

Part II: OWI Pedagogy and Administrative Decisions

This section deals with OWI in the fully online course, in the online writing lab, in considering course logistics, and in the involvement of contingent labor, all issues of particular interest to WPAs. In chapter four, Scott Warnock—known for the *Teaching Writing Online: How and Why*—focuses specifically on OWI Principles 2–6 framed around pedagogy for the online writing course (OWC), like responding to student writing and using audio/visual technologies. Some of the information provided by Warnock supports the themes of Snart, Mick, and Middlebrook from Part 1. Particularly, Warnock addresses the importance yet lack of OWI training for WPAs and teachers (referring to Principle 7 and foreshadowing chapter eleven). He also notes that assessment and teacher evaluation are weak points in OWI, addressing these as potential areas for future research. Following the OWC discussion, Diane Martinez and Leslie Olsen (chapter five) overview the various incarnations of Online Writing Labs (OWLs). They discuss how OWLs have ranged from online PDFs to interactive online components. Martinez and Olsen then discuss strategies, challenges, and recommendations for both synchronous and asynchronous tutoring and training that incorporate accessibility and inclusivity.

In chapter six "Administrative Decisions for OWI," Deborah Minter discusses how the WPA in an OWI capacity needs to consider how class size, student preparation, and advocating for resources affect access and inclusivity. WPAs who are toggling responsibilities in face-to-face (f2f) writing instruction and OWI will also need to pay attention to what Griffin and Minter (2013) term the *literacy load*, which is the amount of reading and writing required of students in a course for OWC, as a concern when structuring these opportunities to learn and develop OWC outcomes (153).

Finishing out the section, Mahli Mechenbier (chapter seven) addresses the needs of contingent faculty in OWI. Acknowledging the low pay and lack of training for OWC, Mechenbier makes a few recommendations, like making sure that OWI teachers are receiving the appropriate technological and pedagogical training *prior* (emphasis added) to receiving on OWC assignment, perhaps instituting a mentoring program to encourage professional development in OWI and hiring the best fit for the OWC. These are issues that also materialize within the f2f sections but are complicated by the OWC with the addition of new learning and digital structures as well as pedagogical differences that are involved with OWI.

Part III: Practicing Inclusivity in OWI

While accessibility and inclusivity are incorporated into each chapter throughout the collection, this particular section introduces three underrepresented groups of OWI: students with physical and learning disabilities, multilingual students, and nontraditional students (which includes working class students; older adult students; remotely rural students; urban students; military learners, including both veteran and active duty; and incarcerated students).

Sushil K. Oswal (chapter eight), Susan K. Miller-Cochran (chapter nine), and Michael W. Gos (chapter ten) all admit that the foci of their three chapters require more OWI research. In his chapter, Sushil K. Oswal argues that understanding the Position Statement of Principles "will [alone] not make our OWCs accessible" (259). Upon reading part three, I agree with Oswal's statement. Making our OWCs accessible will certainly necessitate more scholarly research into the needs of these various student populations. It will also require WPAs and OWI teachers advocating at the institutional level on behalf of students and other OWI teachers to acquire the needed resources (which was a theme common among many chapters in this collection) for providing effective learning spaces, often a daunting task for f2f writing courses.

As a reader, I was struck by how each of these chapters about these individual student/writer populations could have been, and should have been, a collection on its own to really do the students/writers' and authors' ideas justice. Unlike other chapters within the collection, this particular section presents discussions that OWI teachers and institutions grapple with the most due to the lack of discipline-specific research, lack of resources, and institutional stigmatization. Even though I may not have as many answers or successful examples and evidence of initiatives after reading these three chapters, I was provided with recommendations and the beginnings of discussions that will certainly foster further investigation and exploration at my institution in terms of need and resources. This section demonstrates the large gap in research for us to have deeper conversations for the "fundamental attitudinal shift" that Oswal calls for in his chapter (259).

Part IV: Faculty and Student Preparation in OWI

For those who have already been in the trenches of OWI, this section provides readers, particular WPAs, with some concrete examples of activities to implement in their OWI training programs. In "Faculty Preparation for OWI," Lee-Ann Kastman Breuch (chapter eleven), offers a 4-M Training Approach: migration, model, modality and media, and morale, along with several examples of practical activities to use during training to facilitate 4-M. To continue on the preparedness of faculty in OWI, in chapter twelve, Rich Rice argues that current models of professional development have not met the expectations of the "newness of OWI as a disciplinary approach" (389); therefore, he offers a few different software development models of professionalization (code and fix, predictive updating and assessment, agile design) to the OWI effective principles. He asserts that professional development needed to adapt is time intensive and focuses on the individual (407–08).

In "Preparing Students for OWI," Lisa Meloncon and Heidi Harris (chapter thirteen) utilize CCCC OWI Committee survey data to recommend institutional level initiatives (that also hark back to the need for teacher training and resources) and instructor level actions (that also address the concerns of the underrepresented student populations acknowledged in Part 3). As is the case with Breuch, Meloncon and Harris also provide specific, effective, and reasonable activities that can be considered and implemented by the reader. Bringing together preparation for teachers and students, Kevin Eric DePew (chapter fourteen) calls for teachers to become "digital rhetoricians" (457) and for students to become "practitioners of digital rhetoric" (459), compos[ers] of "linguistic and multimodal texts," and aware of how "the technology [used in OWI] influences the text they want to compose" (461).

Taken alone, DePew's chapter may seem overwhelming; however, when considering the NCTE Definition of 21st Century Literacies, the NCTE Position Statement on Multimodal Literacies, digital rhetoric and pedagogy scholarship by Cynthia L. Selfe, among many others, or even chapters fifteen and sixteen in this collection, DePew is drawing a deeper connection between OWI and existing research in the field of Composition and Rhetoric.

Part V: New Directions in OWI

Expanding DePew's call for the OWC to become of place for rhetorical preparation, the reader is provided with Kristine L. Blair's chapter (chapter fifteen) about multimodality and Rochelle Rodrigo's chapter (chapter sixteen) on mobile devices. In "Teaching Multimodal Assignments in OWI Contexts," Blair acknowledges the challenges and obstacles (i.e., faculty engagement, training, LMS limitations) and offers possibilities of how the combination of OWI and multimodality can facilitate 21st century students' critical thinking skills and promote navigation through the various reading and composing processes required of them now. Blair then offers and recommends various assignments, approaches, and assessments that can be implemented in the multimodal OWC. In "OWI on the Go," Rochelle Rodrigo explores the importance of mobile devices to our students and lack of discipline-specific research into how students are completing work and interacting in OWCs using their mobile devices. She notes several problems currently that WPAs should be aware of and consider, all of which I have placed in question form below:

- How, or do, LMS apps/course design equal workable spaces with use of mobile devices?
- How are students who are using primarily mobile devices completing high stakes assignments, such as research essays?
- How can LMS apps and course design provide user friendly work spaces with use of mobile devices?

Rodrigo discusses each of the aforementioned situations and makes recommendations for the inclusion of mobile pedagogy, professional development, and institutional support as considerations to OWI preparation and OWC outcomes, making an argument for these as literacy opportunities and new learning spaces.

Following the two chapters by Blair and Rodrigo, Christa Ehmann and Beth L. Hewett's chapter (chapter seventeen), "OWI Research Considerations," continues in the "new directions" vein, posing concerns and needs from the earlier chapters and presenting additional questions and gaps in the scholarship by suggesting OWI avenues for further research. Concluding the collection, Beth L. Hewett and Scott Warnock in their chapter (chapter eighteen) entitled, "The Future of OWI," state that "The future of OWI is not down the road. It is *now*" (549; emphasis original). This sense of immediacy is due to the nature of the publication process and that technology continues to evolve at a rate that supersedes the rate it enters the academe. They conclude the chapter, and the collection, with a discussion of what "good OWI" means (providing seven points and discussion) and argue how OWI ultimately assists the field of composition "to a new place," (561) within the field's history, scholarship, and alignment with digital scholarship. By grounding the entire collection in access and inclusivity, the authors and editors are showing the potential of these digital venues and genres to increase students' literacies, thereby opening up opportunities for critical investigation.

This collection offers what the Peterson and Savenye's special issue of *Computers and Composition Distance Education: Promises and Perils of Teaching and Learning Online* did for me over a decade ago, but stronger and more entrenched in discipline-specific research: a presence of an online community of support, thoughtful research, and validation of issues that are ongoing at my institution. The authors and editors of this collection recognize "that developing an increasingly critical perspective on technological literacy and technology issues is a responsibility of our profession," especially in online learning (Selfe 151).

Yet, as celebrated by many of the authors, OWI teachers are first teachers of writing, and as Warnock notes in his chapter, OWI principles do not represent an out-of-the-box recipe for teaching composition online (177), which is appropriate because the content of this collection does not provide a specific how-to but offers suggestions, considerations, and examples. *Foundational* is an appropriate word in this collection's title because of the breadth of topics covered and the range of effective principles in action. By providing questions throughout and by highlighting some of the potentials of OWI—i.e., more access/inclusiveness, training, assessment, MOOCs/MOOEEs, literacy development, multimodality, mobile learning—the authors provide an underpinning for future research and encourage further implementation the CCCC OWI principles.

Works Cited

CCCC OWI Committee for Effective Practices in Online Writing Instruction. *A Position Statement of Principles and Effective Practices for Online Writing Instruction (OWI)*. NCTE, 13 March 2013. Web. 23 November 2015.

Griffin, June, and Deborah Minter. "The Rise of the Online Writing Classroom: Reflecting on the Material Conditions of College Composition Teaching." *College Composition and Communication* 65.1 (2013): 140–61. Print.

Multimodal Literacies Issue Management Team. *Position Statement on Multimodal Literacies*. NCTE, Nov. 2005. Web. 22 Dec. 2015.

The NCTE Definition of 21st Century Literacies. NCTE, Feb. 2013. Web. 22 Dec. 2015.

Peterson, Patricia Webb, and Wilhelmina Savenye, eds. *Distance Education: Promises and Perils of Teaching and Learning Online*. Spec. Issue of *Computers and Composition* 18.4 (2001): 319–430. Print.

Selfe, Cynthia L. *Technology and Literacy in the Twenty-First Century: The Importance of Paying Attention*. Carbondale: Southern Illinois UP, 1999. Print.

Warnock, Scott. *Teaching Writing Online: How and Why*. Urbana: NCTE, 2009. Print.

Elizabeth A. Monske is Associate Professor and Director of Composition at Northern Michigan University, a four-year public comprehensive university. Her teaching responsibilities include technical communication, composition and rhetoric, and OWI pedagogy. She has published in Computers and Composition, Kairos, The Journal of Literacy and Technology, *and the* Journal of Educational Technology and Society. *With Dr. Kristine L. Blair, she has a co-edited collection under contract with IGI Global,* Writing and Composing in the Age of MOOCs. *Dr. Monske has also presented scholarship and given workshops on issues related to digital identity, eportfolios, composition, and academic service learning at numerous national conferences.*

Review

A Bird's Eye View of WAC in Practice: WAC Writing Assignments at 100 Colleges and Universities

Emily Isaacs

Mezler, Dan. *Assignments Across the Curriculum*. Logan: Utah State UP, 2014. Print. 148 pages.

In this lucid, insightful, and ultimately praxis-oriented monograph, Dan Melzer provides a view of the state of WAC writing assignments in postsecondary education in the US through an empirical method that emphasizes the bird's eye view over the worm's eye view, a method that has been relied upon at least since Warner Taylor sent a freshman English survey to representatives at 232 colleges and universities in 1927. Large scale studies that focus specifically on practices in WAC have been conducted periodically (McLeod, "Strengthening" and "Writing Across the Curriculum"; Thaiss and Porter), with researchers typically coming to the conclusion that WAC as a movement has grown in influence and impact despite significant difficulties: "[T]he record of the past twenty years, replete with its own periodic recessions, has been of growth for WAC, and the current statistics bode well for a healthy, if not always illness-free, future" (Thaiss and Porter 563). Melzer's research is similar to Taylor's and Thaiss and Porter's—and many other surveyors—in his bird's eye efforts, but it differs in that his primary interest is to understand genre and the rhetorical context of the writing assignments students face after first-year composition and in his avoidance of the survey methodology.

With the affordances offered by the Internet, and following Chris Anson's call for large-scale research in writing that addresses the fundamental questions of disciplinary writing, *Assignments Across the Curriculum* provides insight into the state of writing across the curriculum by looking closely at 400 writing assignments at 100 postsecondary institutions in the

US. Melzer's findings include those that are to be expected, if not always welcomed, as well as those that should surprise readers. In the expected category, he finds that assignments located within a WAC program are vastly superior to those that are not. In WAC programs, students often write in a variety of genres and rhetorical situations with professors providing support for writing through process pedagogies. Unfortunately, if predictably, his study also documents instructors' continued focus on grammatical correctness and an allegiance to the thesis-driven formal essay as a templated form, characteristics that exist in writing assignments from across level, institutional type, and disciplinary focus. Unexpected lowlights include Melzer's finding that, overwhelmingly, students most typically are asked to write to an audience of teacher-as-examiner and to write for the purpose of informing a reader, contradicting a WAC assumption that "students face more rhetorically complex writing tasks as they move from first-year to graduation" (104). However, Melzer's analysis also reveals that while research papers are common, these assignments are more often than not "alternative research writing assignments"—argumentative, personal, essay-form, and multi-genre/media/disciplinary/cultural (Davis and Shadle 418)—presenting "students with rich social contexts and complex, discipline-specific ways of making knowledge" (110). As these highlights are intended to suggest, Melzer's careful analysis of writing assignments provides readers with a rich and detailed portrait of writing across the curriculum courses in practice.

In designing his study, Melzer eschewed the survey with its problem of self-selection bias in favor of a sample that was selected for geographic dispersity and representation of four different types of institutions: doctoral/research, master's comprehensive, baccalaureate colleges, and two-year AA colleges. After selecting institutions, Melzer used the colleges' search engines to select the first syllabus that was listed in each of the following categories: natural sciences, social sciences, business, and humanities. Once the sample had been selected, Melzer more fully investigated each course, finding writing assignments and related documents, ultimately collecting 2,101 writing assignments for his review and analysis. Melzer's method allowed him to include only writing assignments from courses that were published online, and, of course, his bird's eye view precludes a view of the classroom context of any assignment: the commentary and question and answer dialogue that typically occurs when instructors introduce assignments. As Melzer notes, despite these and other limitations, and though the sample is neither randomly selected nor large enough to enable him to make claims "about all of college writing in the United States" (7), his findings are suggestive of trends, complementing the view afforded by longitudinal studies like Herrington and Curtis's *Persons in Process*, Sternglass's *Time to*

Know Them, and Beaufort's *Writing in College and Beyond*. Indeed, given that many of Melzer's insights are based on characteristics that are seen in the vast majority of assignments he has studied, it is easy to be convinced that he has identified significant trends.

In the first two chapters, Melzer situates his study within those that preceded and inspired him, drawing especially on James Britton et al.'s 1975 study of writing completed by students in British secondary schools. Following Britton, Melzer focuses on understanding the rhetorical situation of the writing expected from the assignments he studies, classifying these assignments under the following genres: expressive, poetic, transactional, and exploratory (10). In chapter two, Melzer convincingly (if dishearteningly) presents the case that the genre of choice is almost always transactional, regardless of whether the assignment is located in a lower- or upper-division course or at an elite institution or a community college. What is more, he finds very few expressive or poetic writing assignments. Comparing his discoveries to those from the Harvard Writing Study of Undergraduate Writing (Sommers and Saltz), Melzer states: "In contrast to Sommers and Saltz's (2004) findings regarding Harvard instructors' emphasis on writing as constructing new knowledge through research . . . at the 'elite' colleges in my study, 69% of writing was to inform" (21–22). Notably, Sommers and Saltz's study methodology was different: Perhaps through the addition of interviews with students and teachers, a different view is seen. These differences underscore the imperative that we pursue research questions through a wide variety of methodologies.

For me, a highlight of Melzer's findings is in chapter three when he takes on the research paper, that genre that compositionists generally dislike, but which, we had thought, the rest of the academic world adored (though see Burstein et al. for a sense of the scope of research writing that is assigned in K–12 as well as postsecondary education). For Melzer, the research paper is ubiquitous, but it's more varied and better than he had expected. Classifying a majority of research papers as "alternative," following Davis and Shadle, Melzer provides several examples, one of which I briefly excerpt here:

> Integration Project: As an integration course, cross-cultural psychology seeks to involve students in exploring the interrelationships between two or more disciplines. The purpose of the project is to help you do just that. The format of the project is open to your creative ideas as long as the project looks at culture from two or more disciplinary perspectives. (45)

The instructor lays out several options, demonstrating an appreciation for a diversity of research methods and genres. I will say that a great feature of this book is the excerpts from the writing assignments Melzer has pored over. In these excerpts, we not only see evidence for his claims, but we also get ideas for assignments and fuel for the kinds of faculty development workshops that Melzer recommends and which WPAs, writing fellows, and others with opportunity to work directly in WAC programming would want to develop.

Chapter five is devoted to a close examination of those courses that are affiliated with a WAC initiative. Notably, there are only 12 writing-intensive courses among the sample of 400, but Melzer pays close attention to these courses, observing that they are fundamentally different from the rest. First, these courses are writing intensive; second, these courses involve much more journal writing and more emphasis on writing as a process, including pre-writing activities, peer review, and instructor commentary. In these courses, the average number of assignments per course is 8.7, compared to 5.25 in the whole sample (74). In the WAC courses, Melzer sees "the transformative effects WAC initiatives—like writing-intensive courses or writing fellows programs—have on college instructors and on the literacy expectations placed on student writers" (100). The courses profiled are appealing and testament to the value of WAC, though that there are so few of them and the overall sample is so markedly different gives support to David Russell's quite gloomy prognosis for the possibilities of WAC: "[W]ithout structural changes to integrate writing into the disciplinary fiber of institutions, without a permanent change in the way academics value writing in pedagogy, WAC programs will always work against the grain" (304).

Dan Melzer's book will be of broad interest given the enduring interest in WAC and the interest in genre studies; however, it is also the case that Melzer speaks directly to those of us who run first-year composition programs and writing centers. With his observation of the overwhelming presence of the "writing to inform" genres, Melzer suggests that FYC might be where students could be given opportunity to write "for expressive and poetic purposes" (115). In addition, drawing on his observation that writing assignments across disciplines are actually very similar in their focus on "modes of discourse like 'explaining' or 'defining' or 'arguing'" (119), Melzer suggests that rather than attempt to teach so-called disciplinary genres, FYC instructors should teach students genre, rhetorical, and discourse community awareness, advice that few would argue with, but which is certainly easier said than done. Similarly, he reaches out to writing centers, suggesting that they too focus on "the assignment of the genre and the discourse community the assignment is situated in" (129). Melzer, with deep roots in both FYC and writing centers, makes the case that these concentrated areas of writing expertise can be better utilized to strengthen writing in the disciplines. Melzer concludes that the hard work of increasing the impact of WAC is worthwhile as it is fundamentally a "reform movement" (131), capable of moving us beyond the teacher-centered model and toward an activity-based, genre-diverse approach that makes room for writing in school to be the rich, knowledge-generating, and disseminating activity that those of us who are fortunate enough to be engaged workers, citizens, and sentient humans know it to be.

Works Cited

Anson, Chris. "Toward a Multidimensional Model of Writing in the Academic Disciplines." *Advances in Writing Research*. Vol 2 of *Writing in Academic Disciplines*. Ed. David Joliffe. Norwood: Ablex, 1988. 1–33. Print.

Beaufort, Anne. *College Writing and Beyond: A New Framework for University Writing Instruction*. Logan: Utah State UP, 2007. Print.

Britton, James, Tony Burgess, Nancy Martin, Alex McLeon, Harold Rosen. *The Development of Writing Abilities (11-18)*. London: Macmillan, 1975. Print.

Burstein, Jill, Norbert Elliot, and Hillary Molloy. "Informing Automated Writing Evaluation Using the Lens of Genre: Two Studies." *CALICO Journal* 33.1 (2016): 1–25. Print.

Davis, Robert, and Mark Shadle. "'Building a Mystery': Alternative Research Writing and the Academic Act of Seeking." *College Composition and Communication* 51.3 (2000): 417–46. Print.

Herrington, Anne J., and Marcia Curtis. *Persons in Process: Four Stories of Writing and Personal Development in College*. Urbana: NCTE, 2000. Print.

McLeod, Susan, ed. *Strengthening Programs for Writing across the Curriculum*. 1988. CO: WAC Clearinghouse Landmark Publications in Writing Studies, 2002. 19 Mar. 2002. Web. 29 Dec. 2015.

—. "Writing across the Curriculum: An Introduction." *Writing across the Curriculum: A Guide to Developing Programs*. 1992. Ed. Susan McLeod and Margot Soven. CO: WAC Clearinghouse Landmark Publications in Writing Studies, 2000. 1–8. 23 Aug. 2000. Web. 29 Dec. 2015.

Melzer, Dan. *Assignments Across the Curriculum: A National Study of College Writing*. Logan: Utah State UP, 2014. Print.

Russell, David R. *Writing in the Academic Disciplines, 1870–1990: A Curricular History*. 2nd ed. Carbondale: Southern Illinois UP, 2002. Print.

Sommers, Nancy, and Laura Saltz. "The Novice as Expert: Writing the Freshman Year." *College Composition and Communication* 56.1 (2004): 124–49. Print.

Sternglass, Marilyn. *Time to Know Them: A Longitudinal Study of Writing and Learning at the College Level*. Mahwah: Lawrence Erlbaum Associates, 1997. Print.

Taylor, Warner. "A National Survey of Conditions in Freshman English." *Bureau of Educational Research Bulletin* 11 (1929): 1–44. Print.

Thaiss, Chris, and Tara Porter. "The State of WAC/WID in 2010: Methods and Results of the US Survey of the International WAC/WID Mapping Project." *College Composition and Communication* 61.3 (2010): 534–70. Print.

Emily Isaacs is Associate Dean of Humanities and Social Sciences at Montclair State University, a public research university. In her research, she assesses innovations in writing pedagogy and delivery and examines trends in writing instruction and writing program administration at universities and colleges across the nation. Recently completed projects include a study of writing instructional and programming practices at US state comprehensive universities and an assessment of course redesign projects sponsored by the National Center for Academic Transformation. Her book, Intersections, *co-written with Catherine Keohane, is forthcoming.*

bedford st.martin's
Macmillan Learning

To request your complimentary review copy now, please visit: **macmillanhighered.com/English**

Get involved.

In 1984, we published *The Bedford Bibliography for Teachers of Writing*, the first resource of its kind in the field of rhetoric and composition. Today everything we make is still built to meet the needs of a growing field and changing classroom. We are proud to work with accomplished teachers and scholars who bring their ideas to the classroom in innovative and engaging ways. Join us as we celebrate the work that teachers and students do.

Come join our community to see what's new and to start a conversation.

community.macmillan.com

Professional Resources

Because teaching is central to composition, Bedford/St. Martin's supports the work that teachers do with something for everyone — from the first-time teaching assistant to the program director.

Writer's Help 2.0

**Students get help.
Instructors see progress.**

We asked 1,600 students how they search for help with writing problems: We built our smart search with their responses in mind. Writer's Help 2.0 gives reliable results even when students aren't familiar with composition terms and instead use terms like *flow, point,* or *getting unstuck.* With comprehensive content from authors you trust, Writer's Help 2.0 is an online writing resource that answers writers' questions and lets instructors track student achievement.

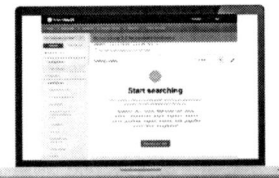

**Writer's Help 2.0
Hacker Version**
writershelp.com/
hacker

Diana Hacker, *late of Prince George's Community College*

Stephen A Bernhardt,
University of Delaware

Nancy Sommers,
Harvard University

**Writer's Help 2.0
Lunsford Version**
writershelp.com/
lunsford

Andrea A. Lunsford,
Stanford University

Get involved. **community.macmillan.com**

NC STATE UNIVERSITY

Master's-Level Study in Rhetoric and Composition at NC State

NC State's Master of Arts in English offers a concentration in Rhetoric and Composition that provides focused study of writing and literacies, the teaching of writing, and the role of persuasive language in academic disciplines, professional and civic life, and culture at large. The concentration offers a flexible curriculum, a nationally recognized faculty, and an award-winning GTA program.

Our MA program is situated in a vibrant intellectual community that also includes an MS degree in Technical Communication, an interdisciplinary Graduate Certificate in Digital Humanities, and an interdisciplinary PhD in Communication, Rhetoric, and Digital Media. Collaboration among these programs yields a rich mix of faculty and student interests and expertise. MA Rhet/Comp students gain a firm theoretical foundation in both composition and rhetoric and also have opportunities to study such areas of interest as

Composition research and pedagogy I Writing and new media
Experimental and multimodal composition I Writing across the curriculum
Rhetorical history and criticism I Sociolinguistics
Professional writing I Scientific and technical communication
Writing program administration

Faculty in Writing and Rhetoric

Chris Anson I Helen Burgess I Michael Carter I David Covington I Stan Dicks I Huiling Ding
Casie Fedukovich I Susan Katz I Hans Kellner I Ann Penrose I Stacey Pigg
David Rieder I Jason Swarts

Learn more at http://english.chass.ncsu.edu/graduate/ma/rhetcomp/

NC State. Think and do.

PARLOR PRESS
EQUIPMENT FOR LIVING

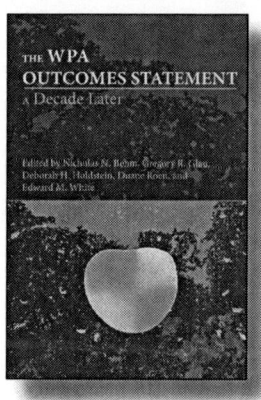

Congratulations to These Award Winners & WPA Scholars!

The WPA Outcomes Statement—A Decade Later
Edited by Nicholas N. Behm, Gregory R. Glau, Deborah H. Holdstein, Duane Roen, and Edward M. White
Winner of the Best Book Award, Council of Writing Program Adminstrators (July, 2015)

GenAdmin: Theorizing WPA Identities in the Twenty-First Century
Colin Charlton, Jonikka Charlton, Tarez Samra Graban, Kathleen J. Ryan, & Amy Ferdinandt Stolley
Winner of the Best Book Award, Council of Writing Program Adminstrators (July, 2014)

Mics, Cameras, Symbolic Action: Audio-Visual Rhetoric for Writing Teachers
Bump Halbritter
Winner of the Distinguished Book Award from *Computers and Composition* (May, 2014)

New Releases

Antiracist Writing Assessment Ecologies: Teaching and Assessing Writing for a Socially Just Future
Asao B. Inoue. 345 pages.

Inoue helps teachers understand the unintended racism that often occurs when teachers do not have explicit antiracist agendas in their assessments.

First-Year Composition: From Theory to Practice
Edited by Deborah Coxwell-Teague & Ronald F. Lunsford. 420 pages.

Twelve of the leading theorists in composition studies answer, in their own voices, the key question about what they hope to accomplish in a first-year composition course. Each chapter includes sample syllabi.

www.parlorpress.com

Extending an invitation to join the

Council of

Writing Program Administrators

The Council of Writing Program Administrators offers a national network of scholarship and support for leaders of college and university writing programs.

Membership benefits include the following:

- A subscription to *WPA: Writing Program Administration*, a semi-annual refereed journal
- Invitations to the annual WPA Summer Workshops and Conferences
- Invitations to submit papers for sessions that WPA sponsors at MLA and CCCC
- Participation in the WPA Research Grant Program, which distributes several awards, ranging from $1000 to $2000
- Invitations to the annual WPA breakfast at CCCC and the annual WPA party at MLA
- Information about the WPA Consultant-Evaluator program

ANNUAL DUES
Graduate Students: $20
Not on Tenure Track: $20
Regular: $40
Sustaining (voluntary): $60
Library: $80

TO JOIN
Visit us online at http://wpacouncil.org/membership or send your name, address, email address, institutional affiliation, and dues to

Michael McCamley, CWPA Secretary
University of Delaware
Department of English
212 Memorial Hall
Newark, DE 19716
mccamley@udel.edu

CPSIA information can be obtained
at www.ICGtesting.com
Printed in the USA
FFOW05n2227200616